HOW TO BE

THE BES
CHRISTIAN STUDY
GROUP LEADER

EVER IN THE WHOLE HISTORY OF THE UNIVERSE

ISRAEL GALINDO

HOW TO BE
THE BEST
CHRISTIAN STUDY
GROUP LEADER
EVER IN THE WHOLE HISTORY OF THE UNIVERSE

JUDSON PRESS
PUBLISHERS SINCE 1824
VALLEY FORGE

How to Be the Best Christian Study Group Leader
Ever in the Whole History of the Universe

Library of Congress Cataloging-in-Publication Data

Galindo, Israel.
    How to be the best Christian study group leader ever in the whole history of the universe / Israel Galindo. — 1st ed.
      p. cm.
    Includes bibliographical references.
      ISBN-13: 978-0-8170-1500-8 (pbk. : alk. paper) 1. Christian education of adults. 2. Teaching. 3. Dialogue. 4. Small groups. I. Title.
      BV1488.G35   2006
      268'.434—dc22

Printed in the U.S.A.

First Edition, 2006.

ACKNOWLEDGMENTS

Thanks to the following friends who took the time to review the manuscript and helped make this a better book: Barbara Massey, Bob Dibble, Burdette Robinson, Greg Randall, Jean Matthews, Jon Messer, Mark Price, Terry Maples, Vanessa Ellison, and, always, Barbara. Thanks to Randy Frame, who made this one possible.

130108

CONTENTS

INTRODUCTION

I think I know something about you. Chances are you have been a part of a small group at some time in your life. And if you have picked up this book, chances are you have been asked to lead, or currently are leading, a small group. If you are just starting to facilitate or lead a small group, you are probably anxiously wondering how to go about doing so. You likely are enthusiastic and eager to begin, and you want to be the best group leader you can be to help your learners have a meaningful and gratifying experience with you as their teacher. If you are a veteran teacher and small group leader, you may have reached the point where you are not satisfied with how you have been teaching. You may be frustrated with how difficult it seems to engage group members in learning. And if you are a teacher who is passionate about what you are teaching, you may be wondering if the problem is with you or with your learners. The purpose of this book is to help you become an effective leader and teacher of adult small study groups.

There are many types of small groups—task groups, support groups, spiritual direction groups, and reading groups, for example. This book is about one particular kind of small group. First, it is a book for Christian groups. Educator and author Roberta Hestenes defines a Christian small group this way: "A Christian small group can be defined as a deliberate face-to-face gathering of three to twelve people who meet regularly and share the common purpose of exploring together some aspect of Christian faith and discipleship."[1]

Effective Christian educators acknowledge that there is a distinctiveness to teaching for faith. Faith, the means by which one lives the Christian life, is not like everything else—it is a particular thing that needs to be learned in particular ways. The teaching methods most effective for spiritual development are relational ones—those that are experiential, personal, and interactive. In addition, authentic Christian teaching takes place in the context of a faith community. One of the great truths about spiritual growth is that we can't go it alone.[2]

A change in teaching style can often mean the difference between students learning or not learning. Changing the way we teach is not easy. Unless we take a course on teaching or intentionally work on our skills, most of us teach the way we have experienced being taught—regardless of how effective that actually was. But a number of learning processes that are possible only in small groups can foster the kind of learning that brings about change in the life of the learner, and this is how I am defining learning in this context—learning is change. Any content information you need to give your learners can efficiently be taught in a small group. After this, the most important dimension of the small group method—engaging learners in the relational learning process—can be used to great advantage. The goal of the small group must be consistent with the goal of Christian teaching: to help the learner hear and respond to God and others in the context of relationship.[3]

Second, this book is about one particular kind of Christian group: the study group. A study group gathers primarily to learn about something of mutual interest—the Bible, a topic, a book, a theme, an idea, or an issue. In this book you will learn about using a learning approach, called *dialogical learning,* that will help make meaningful learning happen in your small group. Dialogical learning is *a structured, intentional process that leads to insights and deep understanding and, ultimately, application in the life of the learner.* The process of dialogical learning in the small group can work with whatever subject or content you may want to consider, and it can also be used with other types of groups, such as support groups, professional groups, and task groups, for example. This book will help you to be an effective leader of a small study group as follows.

In chapter 1 you will be challenged to assess the effectiveness of your teaching approach and encouraged to rethink what it means to be an effective teacher in the congregational context. You will learn why Christian education often just doesn't work and why a different approach is necessary. Chapter 2 will review how people actually learn in groups and provide you with a foundational understanding of dialogical learning as one of the most effective ways to help people "learn faith." These two chapters offer the rationale you may

Benefits of Using Small Groups

1. Small groups provide the intimate and supportive environment in which learners can feel free to meaningfully share their spiritual life stories.

2. Small groups provide one of the most efficient ways for communicating information and processing ideas. Communication relationships grow exponentially with each person in the group. A group of four persons has twelve communication links in its group, while a group of five has twenty communication relationships. A teacher trying to communicate in a class of fifteen learners will need to work with 210 relationships!

3. In a small group, learners have the opportunity to discover their own reactions to the material that is presented and to reflect on its significance to what is happening in their own lives.

4. Small groups become the mediating and interpreting community for the personal religious experiences of the individual group member. Group members expand the pool of experience and knowledge available to each individual.

5. As the immediate expression of the learner's faith community, the small group can help negotiate the imagery for the learner's individual worldview and life metaphor.[4]

need to challenge yourself to change the way you currently teach, and they will help you appreciate the practical methods outlined in subsequent chapters.

In chapter 3, you will learn about the basic dynamics of small groups, including "group math," group roles, and group formation, and more important, how to use small group dynamics to best help the group become an effective faith-learning environment. Chapter 4 offers guidance on developing questions that facilitate dialogical learning and provides a practical planning tool for preparing questions for your group study. Closely related to developing effective dialogical questions is the ability to design sound dialogical learning objectives. Chapter 5 will help you learn how to design or select objectives that lead to meaningful learning.

Chapter 6 catalogs, explains, and illustrates learning methods that are most suitable for small group study using the dialogical learning approach. In this chapter you will find a repertoire of methods that are leader directed but learner focused and suitable for most subject matter. Finally, chapters 7, 8, and 9 provide a variety of examples of the dialogical learning approach to small group study. Chapter 7 presents two sample sessions of the approach for use in a book study, while chapter 8 shows how to lead an effective, goal-oriented dialogical Bible study and chapter 9 offers an example of a topical Bible study that uses the dialogical learning approach in the small group context. Finally, the appendices provide practical tools and resources you can use for review, practice, or information. Be sure to refer to them as directed.

PART 1
Dialogical Learning

CHAPTER 1

Why Christian Education Doesn't Matter

For years I have tried to understand why people seem not to learn much in Sunday school or in other church educational programs—despite dedicated teachers and sincere and hardworking staff, a multitude of programs, hours spent in classes and workshops by intelligent and motivated participants, adequate facilities, and a wide range of curriculum choices. Why is it that biblical illiteracy remains so rampant in our churches? How is it that people can attend Sunday school for years and not show evidence of spiritual growth? Why is it that people can read and study the Bible in church yet not live biblically?

In 1999, for example, the Associated Press reported that in at least one major denomination there is a disconnect between the ideal and the reality. "Baptists have the highest divorce rate of any Christian denomination, and are more likely to get a divorce than atheists and agnostics, according to a national survey."[1] Apparently, biblical teaching about divorce or the sanctity of marriage makes no difference in the lives of a significant number of believers!

What is the reason Christians cannot seem to apply what they learn about faith and about being a Christian on Sunday morning or Wednesday evening, for example, to their lives and relationships on Monday or Thursday? Decades ago the writer and educator Morton

Kelsey wrote a book titled *Can Christians Be Educated?*[2] Sometimes it seems that the answer to that question is, "It appears not."

The Deadly Null-Expectancy Factor

I think I have stumbled on the reason why so much of what passes for Christian education in congregations is so ineffective and, therefore, why Christian education probably doesn't matter much in the lives of our church members. I call it "the deadly null-expectancy factor." By this phrase, I mean that the ways we often teach in our congregations ensure that Christians have no expectation of actually learning anything, or if they do learn something, they have no expectation that what they learn will have direct application to their lives—at work, at home, or on a personal level. Christian education doesn't matter because we do it in a way that is inconsistent with how people actually learn faith.

Admittedly, church members enjoy learning about the Bible and about spiritual matters. Many members faithfully attend church educational events. They love their teachers and genuinely enjoy being with other church members. All evidence indicates that churches have increased in-house educational offerings to include everything from Bible studies to church officer training to classes on marriage and parenting. Most educators agree that the basic definition of learning is change, and unfortunately, all indications are that participation does not ensure learning.

If Christian education is about anything, it is about helping persons change in a particular way—that is, to mature in their faith, or, as the apostle Paul put it in his letter to the Ephesians, to grow "to maturity, to the measure of the full stature of Christ" (4:13). In many cases, participation in Christian education does not foster those things that are most important in the Christian life, namely, a deep understanding of the Bible; growth in character and grace; an increased capacity to love God, self, and others; engagement in ministry and mission; and an overall increased commitment to living as a disciple of Jesus, as one conformed to the mind and Spirit of Christ.

When I say that Christian education doesn't matter, I don't mean to imply that Christian education is not important. I think it is *very* important. In fact, effective Christian education is critically important in helping Christians mature in faith. According to a 1999 Search Institute study, "Christian education matters more than we expected. Of all the areas of congregational life we examined, involvement in an effective Christian education program has the strongest tie to a person's growth in faith and to loyalty to one's congregation and denomination. While other congregational factors also matter, nothing matters more than effective Christian education."[3] In case you missed it, the operative word in that quote is "effective." *How* we tend to go about educating people in faith is so often ineffective that Christian education is a benign endeavor—that is, one that makes no real difference in how people live.

If you have trouble accepting these dire notions, consider trying one of the following activities.

1. To test the lowest level of learning, which is recall of information, give participants the Basic Bible Quiz (appendix A).

2. To test comprehension through the ability to understand and explain terms, have your group divide into pairs or threes and assign each person one of the following terms: faith, redemption, justification, justice, peace, mercy, hope, trust, salvation, revelation, love, grace, or repentance. Ask each person to (a) define the term, (b) give an example of what it means, (c) give an example of what it does *not* mean, and (d) describe an application of the concept.

3. To test how relevant Christian education is in members' lives and how able they are to apply what they learn, interview several church members who regularly attend church educational events. Ask them to share how their church education experience has helped them grow in their faith and in their personal lives. Ask specifically how church education has helped in their relationships and family life, at work, in life decisions, and in their relationship with God. Push for specifics, ask for examples, and challenge them to get past superficial "Sunday school answers," then ask what has helped *most* over the years in dealing with family, work, and other relationships.

The results may be sobering. You may indeed confirm the chilling revelation that people seem not to have learned much about the Bible in church, people cannot articulate fundamental concepts of faith, and what has made the most difference in people's lives, what has influenced their decisions about daily living, has not been what they learned through church education programs. You may be left asking the uncomfortable question, what have we been doing all these years?

CAUSES OF THE NULL-EXPECTANCY FACTOR

It seems, then, that we have found a way to defeat our purpose of making disciples and helping people mature in their faith. How did this come about? One cause is that we have gone about educating Christians the wrong way. We have chosen to "school" people in faith. By "schooling," I mean ways of teaching and learning that are primarily instructional, content-focused, and teacher-centered, and that take place in the context of a classroom setting that rigidly prescribes the roles of "teacher" and "student." Schooling can be effective in helping people learn *about* concepts and ideas related to faith, but learning about faith is very different from acquiring faith, experiencing faith, or growing in the life of faith. People don't learn faith through schooling, and a very real danger is that if schooling is the primary approach to church education, members may inadvertently

---

Ways That Schooling Perpetuates the Deadly Null-Expectancy Factor

- creates an overdependence on the teacher or leader as "expert," keeping the learner a passive and perpetual "novice" in the Christian life

- makes others (the teacher or leader) responsible for one's faith, assuring that the learner won't take responsibility for his or her own growth in faith

- affirms and offers assurance of existing beliefs, rather than challenge, which is the motivation for learning and growth—too many church members hold on to uncritical beliefs from childhood

- equates belief (as in cognitive assent) with faith, which is a lived reality

- fosters passive and dependent learners through teaching-by-telling methods that ensure that learners do not have to think for themselves

- overfocuses on content that is external to the learner rather than on the (personal and corporate) experience of lived faith and making meaning of that experience, which is what spiritual growth is all about

- assumes that content is transformative when, in fact, relationships are formative and mediate spiritual formation

---

acquire the unfortunate assumption that learning *about* faith is tantamount to having and growing in faith. Schooling perpetuates the deadly null-expectancy factor and disregards how adults learn.

How Adults Learn

I love riddles that start with "What's the difference between. . . ?"

Q. *What is the difference between a lawyer and a trampoline?*
A. You take your shoes off before you jump on a trampoline.

Or,

Q. *What is the difference between a clarinet and an onion?*
A. Nobody cries when you chop up a clarinet.

So here's an educational one:

Q. *What's the difference between a child learner and an adult learner?*
A. Dialogical learning! Because adults learn differently than children.

Well, okay, that one is not as funny as the others, but it's true. Teaching children is very different from teaching adults. That should be obvious, but is it? If we look at the learning methods and approaches we use in most of our adult Christian education opportunities, it seems that we may be teaching adults and children in much the same way!

Andragogy, a theory of adult learning developed by Malcom Knowles, takes seriously the impact of four interrelated characteristics on the adult learning experience. These are *self-concept, experience, readiness to learn,* and *orientation to learning.*[4] Andragogy provides a framework for looking at learning on a continuum, which helps teachers choose appropriate approaches. For example, when learners begin to study a totally new content area, they will be dependent on a teacher until enough content has been acquired to enable self-directed inquiry and exploration. Most adults who enter into a learning situation on a subject they know little about function on the level of a fourteen-year-old, regardless of expertise in other areas. They enter the learning situation unsure of themselves and dependent. Instruction is an appropriate method early on, because the learner needs information, but for meaningful learning, the experience needs to move quickly into a more adult-oriented dimension, like dialogical learning. In other words, a goal of Christian education is to move the learners from novice to competence about the Christian life, not to keep them perpetually dependent and timid. The "Teaching-Learning Assumptions" chart highlights the differences between traditional schooling/instructional approaches and the dialogical learning approaches that are congruent with adult learning.

Teaching-Learning Assumptions

Components and Processes	Schooling/Instruction	Dialogical Learning
Climate	Formal, tense, authority-oriented, competitive	Relaxed, mutually informative, collaborative
Planning	Primarily by the teacher	Collaboratively by group members with group leader
Determination of outcomes	Primarily by the teacher	Collaboratively by group members with group leader
Setting learning goals	Primarily by the teacher	Collaboratively by group members with group leader
Learning methods	Instructional, transmittal, teacher-led, content-driven	Dialogical learning, inquiry, student-focused, experience-centered
Evaluation of learning	By teacher, referenced by criterion	Evidence of learning validated by peers; by group consent

Use the checklist on page 9 to test your teaching approach with adult learners. Do you give attention to andragogical principles in your teaching?

The single most obvious reason children participate in church education is that adults bring them. Children don't drive themselves to church, and given a choice, many may prefer to stay home. They attend because they are brought—sometimes against their will! However, once they are there, participation is genuine for most of them—they like being in church and learning about God, the Bible, self, and the world.

Adults, on the other hand, participate by choice. They will more likely choose to participate in learning opportunities that are immediately relevant to their life situations. Topics or learning opportunities that offer "future" benefits are low motivators. Adults will also participate when they are allowed to actively engage in the learning experience, which is what happens with dialogical learning. Adults need, and want, to talk about their current experiences of life and faith, and they learn both by sharing their stories and hearing the stories of others. One reason adults resist participation in church education is that the learning methods are incongruent with how they need to learn. When adults perceive that the educational experiences offered by the church are not relevant to their lives, they will choose not to participate—even while they feel the need for learning and growth in the life of faith! As one church member expressed it, "The worst thing you can do is waste my time."

Teaching adults often becomes a matter of removing obstacles to participation and moving toward teaching approaches that enable meaningful learning experiences. This means moving from a schooling-classroom approach to a small group dialogical learning approach. The following checklist is a helpful tool for evaluating your current approach to adult teaching.

Adult Teaching Checklist

- [ ] I allow for a relaxed, informal but respectful atmosphere in the group.
- [ ] Planning is by mutual consent of the group members.
- [ ] Objectives for learning outcomes are negotiable.
- [ ] I allow, and challenge, group members to be responsible for their own learning.
- [ ] The teaching methods I use foster independent learning, experiential activities, and dialogical learning.
- [ ] The group learning experience is life- or task-centered.
- [ ] Group members are a resource to each other in the learning experience; they serve as co-teachers as well as co-learners.
- [ ] Evaluation of the effectiveness and meaningfulness of the group learning experience is mutually determined.

The Solution

The solution to the deadly null-expectancy factor is to find a way of educating people in faith that makes for meaningful learning and relevance. To do this, we need to

- move from teacher-focused methods to learner-centered methods
- move from teacher-dependent to learner-motivated learning
- move from content transmission to discovery learning
- move from passive listening to active participation
- move from external-focused learning to internal-focused learning
- move from content-focused instruction to relationship-mediated experiences

Changing the way we teach is difficult, but we must move toward more appropriate ways to teach if we want the experience of learning in church to matter. The diagram on page 11 illustrates how certain methods and approaches work better for meaningful learning and for learning as formation.

The circle represents the congregational context in which education for spiritual formation takes place. Learners within these groups have formative relationships on several levels, including congregational, small group, family, and individual. The dashed line represents the congregation's existence in the context of the world and of a community with which it often shares the values and culture. The dotted line running between the poles of "Schooling" and "Dialogical Learning" represents the continuum of educational approaches. Two basic congregational movements are illustrated as "inviting" those outside the church into its fellowship and "sending" those within the church to engage the world. The corresponding educational movements are what have been traditionally termed "the journey inward" and "the journey outward." A holistic approach to Christian education will facilitate movement in both directions, and in the next chapter, we will explore how dialogical learning can be effective in facilitating each of these movements.

At the center of the diagram appears "Worship & Word" to represent core values that inform the church's mission and vision and, subsequently, shape its understanding of Christian education for the

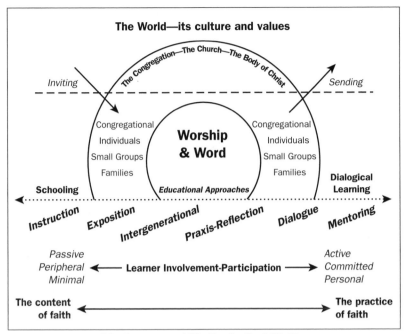

Moving toward Methods that Matter

spiritual formation of participants. It is possible for a church, depending on its theology and identity, to replace this informing center with another core. For example, a church might choose to place at the center worship and fellowship, praise and mission, or proclamation and outreach. It is likely that, where Christian education enterprises are not functional, there is not only a failure in methodology (using the wrong means for the intended ends), but also in a lack of clarity of theology and identity. Indeed, the work of an authentic and viable Christian education begins with a clear sense of a church's core values. If you do not know the theology that informs you as a teacher, how can you decide which methods are most appropriate or discern when a teaching method is not congruent with the goals and values of Christian teaching as you understand it?

The two arrows at the bottom of the diagram illustrate how movement from schooling methods toward dialogical learning affects how students respond to learning. The "Learner Involvement-Participation" line shows that methods such as instruction and exposition yield passive learners, present content that is peripheral to learners, and require minimal participation. As educational approaches such as dialogical learning are used, learners are required to be more active and committed and to personally accept both the content and process of learning. The powerful truth that we must respect here is that the educational enterprise is formative. Consistent exposure to one type of educational approach will produce a particular kind of learner.

Along the "Educational Approaches" line are six examples of learning approaches across the spectrum from schooling to dialogical learning. Any number of teaching methods fall under each approach and reflect the goals and objectives of each. For goals related to mastery of concepts, facts, and Bible content, the methods related to instruction are appropriate (for example, memorizing a Bible verse, recalling a Bible story accurately, identifying where a city is on a map or identifying on a map where a certain Bible story took place, giving a definition for a concept like grace or joy, or being able to state the difference between faith and hope). However, some things in the Christian faith are never learned through instruction—they are learned only in community, through relationships, and by obedience. In much of the Christian life, faith is acquired by obeying *first;* then insight follows obedience.

A steady diet of methods from the approaches on the left side of the chart will produce passive learners who have minimal commitment to the focus and experience of learning. The bottom arrow illustrates that approaches on the left end of the spectrum (for example, instruction) are more concerned with the "content of faith," while those approaches plotted toward the right side of the spectrum (for example, dialogue, and ultimately, learning through obedience) are concerned with the practice of faith. In other words, the methods associated with the approaches on the right side of the spectrum are, in fact, the practices of faith!

Let's recall two scenarios from the Gospels. In the first, a crowd surrounds Jesus—some are followers, some are disciples, and some are merely curious. Jesus, the master teacher, teaches by talking about the birds of the air and the lilies of the field—how they do not toil or work yet God cares for them. He tells them that their loving Father in heaven cares for them even more. He says, therefore, "Do not worry, saying, 'What will we eat?' or 'What will we drink?' or 'What will we wear?'"

(Matthew 6:31). The crowd is inspired. Doubtless, many are moved and others walk away saying, "What a wonderful speaker!"

In the second scene, Jesus gathers his intimate small group of disciples. He sends them on a mission with instructions to "take nothing for their journey except a staff; no bread, no bag, no money in their belts; but to wear sandals and not to put on two tunics" (Mark 6:8-9). The disciples obey and return reporting the great works they were able to do in God's name. Now, here's the important question: Who do you think really learned to trust God? Was it the people in the large crowds who heard a great sermon and were "inspired"? Or was it the *small group* of disciples who, because of their *relationship* with Jesus, and because they *obeyed first*—even without fully understanding—*experienced* God's provision?

Some things in the Christian life are learned only through relationships because relationships mediate growth in the life of faith. And for the kind of relationships that help persons grow in faith in the learning context, dialogical learning is necessary. Using dialogical learning as a primary approach to small group studies, especially Bible study, is a movement toward a more authentic and meaningful way to teach those things that are at the heart of the Christian faith. Dialogical learning will help us shift from passive learning to active engagement, from a peripheral concern with Bible truths to active application, from dependence on others to taking responsibility for our values and convictions.

If we want to make Christian education matter in the lives of our members, we need to move away from instructional approaches that focus on *teaching* and move toward dialogical approaches that emphasize *learning*. To be authentic Christian teachers, the methods we use in Christian education need to be authentically Christian. In the remaining chapters, we will examine how consistently moving toward and using the small group method with a dialogical learning approach can facilitate spiritual formation and meaningful learning.

CHAPTER 2

The Power of
Dialogical Learning

"**I cannot teach anyone anything,** I can only make them think," said the philosopher Socrates.[1] While that may be an overstatement, it is more true than false. I suspect that the first half of Socrates's statement may be the cry of many frustrated church teachers. As mentioned in chapter 1, the reason Christian education doesn't matter in the lives of our church members is because we tend to go about teaching faith in a teaching-by-telling method. You know what this method looks like: the teacher studies and prepares for the lesson, typically in isolation. Then polite but passive learners gather at an appointed time and sit in rows or in a semicircle facing the teacher, who stands in front and attempts to impart knowledge during the 40 to 50 minutes allotted for learning. This is not necessarily a painful or boring experience for the learner. Some teachers can be inspiring, engaging, and entertaining, but it generally results in little or no change, and the point of learning is to *learn*, to be *changed* by what one encounters.

As I mentioned in the introduction, the most basic, accepted definition of learning is "Learning equals change." No change, no learning. Teaching by "telling" does not change learners, because teaching-by-telling does other people's thinking for them. The process of learning is active and dynamic; it requires internal and external processes that bring about change in the way a person thinks, in what he or she values or does. The dynamics of learning include discovery, connection through experience, reflection, awareness of our prejudices, the uncovering of uncritical assumptions and naïveté, achievement of self-understanding, and application. Teaching-by-telling circumvents the learning process by blocking these dynamics.

Additionally, the two greatest motivators for learning are challenge and a perceived or actual need. Teaching-by-telling lets the potential learner off the hook by not addressing either. If the teacher does all the work of thinking, then the learner assumes that he or she does not need to think—no challenge. It does not take long for persons consistently exposed to this style of teaching to assume that the teacher is the one who does all the work. They come to accept themselves as passive recipients of information and of another person's insight gained through his or her hard work. They come to believe that the Christian faith does not require work, thinking, or struggling. And most tragically, they may come to believe that what it means to be a good disciple is to be passive and dependent.

Furthermore, teaching-by-telling focuses more on content than on the needs of learners. Too often we assume that content has meaning in and of itself, but content has meaning only to the extent that a learner perceives that it meets a personal need. With no overt connection between content and personal need, learning is irrelevant. Teaching by telling, therefore, creates unmotivated learners who have a null expectancy about church educational experiences, which makes the work of teaching almost impossible. *How* we teach, matters, and how we teach for *faith* matters more, since the goal is to help learners grow in faith and maturity.

Challenge and discovery learning are better learning approaches for teaching that changes people's lives. The dialogical learning approach is a type of discovery learning that moves the learner from being a passive recipient to being an active participant. In discovery learning through dialogical learning, people work through the processes necessary for gaining insight, and they learn for themselves. We may not be able to teach anybody anything, but as good teachers, we can provide the things that are necessary for people to learn for themselves. These include the right environment, the right attitude, appropriate kinds of knowledge, and the right educational methods.

Domains of Learning

Learning requires change in the learner, and that change happens in one of three domains: (1) the affective, which includes emotions and values; (2) the cognitive, which includes understanding and comprehension; or (3) the behavioral, which includes action and practices. Additionally, people need to *want* to learn and then *choose* to do so, which is represented by a fourth domain—the volitional.[2]

We know someone has really learned something when some kind of change is evidenced, such as a better idea, a deeper understanding, a different attitude, or a new skill. Yet there is a difference between ordinary learning and *meaningful* learning. For example, when we teach matters of Christian belief and faith, we want that learning to be more than trivia. We want that learning to make a difference in the life of the learner. For meaningful learning to happen, all four domains must be operative to some degree. We can say that persons have achieved meaningful learning to the degree that the learning is operative in all four domains of their lives. To the degree that any one of these four key domains is not operative in a person's life, that person has not really "learned," because learning ultimately brings about change in the whole of a person's life. This then is the challenge of integrity for Christian teachers: are we really making a difference in the lives of learners?

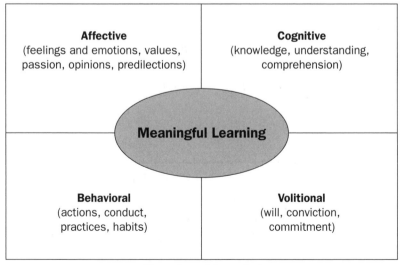

Domains of Learning

If there isn't evidence of change and growth in lives as a result of our teaching, then it is likely we are not teaching for Christian living and that our students are not experiencing meaningful learning.

It is relatively easy to lead learners through the cognitive, affective, and behavioral domains. For example, an experienced teacher can guide a learner through the cognitive stages of recall, comprehension, application, analysis, and evaluation in a single lesson. Likewise, an inspiring teacher can lead students through the stages of the affective domain—from receiving to responding to valuing to organization to characterization—with anticipated success. Changing behavior in students is not difficult either. Whenever someone learns a new skill or a different way of doing something, there is change in the behavioral domain.

Changing behaviors, however, can be deceptive. A change in behavior does not mean there has been a change in belief. In fact, we are so efficient in changing people's behavior by teaching them to "act" like Christians that someone has suggested that the danger in much of Christian education is that we merely teach pagans how to behave as Christians! Again, unless all four domains (the affective, cognitive, behavioral, and volitional) are operative, there is no real belief, no meaningful learning. This may explain, in part, why despite our attempts to address the issue of Christian stewardship in our churches year after year, we rarely see significant change in how people handle stewardship of money, talents, or time.[3] Like technique-based weight-loss diets or informational seminars on how to quit smoking, most stewardship "teaching" addresses the cognitive and the behavioral without addressing the affective and the volitional. Turn to "Stewardship: A Case in Point" on page 24 for a practical illustration of these learning issues.

Of all the domains, the most difficult in which to do "teaching" is the volitional. More than any other, this is the domain of the spirit—not even God over-rides into this domain of human will. God's greatest desire is for us to love God, but God will never coerce us to love God. Love is volitional. We must choose to love, just as we must choose to learn. The effective teacher respects the dynamics of the volitional domain, which are relationship, trust, honesty, openness, and time. The effective teacher also respects the boundaries over which he or she must not cross. No amount of manipulation or technique can make a learner *want* or *will* to learn or to change. This is why deep relationships are so important—relationships are mediators of the volitional.

People have freedom to choose to learn or not to learn, but when they are in deep relationships with others, they often want to learn and choose to learn and grow through those relationships. A common shortcoming in teaching matters of faith is the failure to address matters of volition. Perhaps this is because volition cannot be addressed in a single Bible study session or in the course of a Sunday school quarter. Volition is the domain that requires an intentional commitment from the learner to both the truth he or she encounters and to his or her learning relationships. And herein lies the power of dialogical learning: it facilitates the development of the kind of relationships that mediate the ability to make a choice.

Dialogical Learning and the Nature of Christian Education

Dialogical learning is suited for Christian education in small groups because it taps into all four of the domains of learning in the context of relationships within a community of faith. Dialogue, the foundation of dialogical learning, is not simply talk or conversation or the sharing of ideas and opinions. *It is a structured, intentional process that leads to insights and deep understanding and ultimately to application in the*

Dialogical Learning versus Discussion

Dialogical Learning Seeks

- to inquire and to discover in order to learn from others and self

- to connect with others' perspectives and experiences to discover shared meaning

- to integrate the multiple perspectives in a group

- to uncover and challenge personal assumptions and prejudices

Discussion Seeks

- to tell, persuade, and convince others

- consensus on meaning

- to evaluate and select the "best" perspective

- to affirm, justify, and defend one's assumptions

---

life of the learner. There is a strategic purpose to dialogical learning aimed at leading the learner beyond his or her initial stages of knowledge and belief. All of the domains of learning are addressed so as to bring about change in the learner.

As the chart "Dialogical Learning versus Discussion" on page 19 illustrates, dialogical learning is not the same as "discussion," as most people have experienced it. While discussion seeks to persuade others, dialogue seeks understanding. Dialogue has less to do with certitude and more to do with discovery. While instruction may be fine for a schooling context, the dialogical learning approach to small group study is congruent with the context in which Christian education takes place, namely, a community of faith. The context of a church that is a genuine community of faith requires a different kind of learning—learning in and through relationships with one another. The very nature and context of Christian education supports the notion that dialogical learning in small groups is a more authentic and ultimately a more effective way of teaching disciples of Christ.

Christian teaching is similar to other forms of education in that it helps persons learn, but it is essentially different. Education becomes *Christian* education when it redefines the classic educational categories of context, content, approach, methods, and outcome in distinctive Christian terms. The following chart and discussion compares and contrasts a schooling approach with an authentic Christian education approach.[4]

Educational Categories and Key Questions

Educational Categories and Key Questions	Schooling	Authentic Christian Education
CONTEXT	school or classroom	community of faith
CONTENT	text or creed	person of Jesus Christ
APPROACH	instructional	relational
OUTCOME	mastery of content	becoming while in relationship
METHODS	teach-by-telling	dialogical learning
What is important?	*what* you know	*whom* you know
How are you saved?	by *what* you know	by *the One* you know

The context. The context in which Christian teaching happens is not so much a "classroom" as it is a community of faith, which is what a church *is*. Jesus did not establish a seminary to carry on the work of the gospel. Rather, he sent the Holy Spirit to birth something essentially new and different from anything that ever existed before—what the apostle Paul called a "mystery," namely, the church. A community is where we learn who we are with the help of others, where our vocational identity is not so much found as it is negotiated in conversation with others. Most important, community is where we are mentored and taught the skills of how to make meaning in life.

The content. Traditionally, the answer to the question, "What is the content of Christian education?" is "The Bible." After all, that's what faithful churchgoers grew up studying in Sunday school. I contend, however, that a more legitimate answer is *"The person of Jesus Christ and the learner's relationship with him."* As we examine the New Testament, we discover that its content is the person of Jesus Christ. The Gospels and Epistles are literary samples of the continual struggle to know, understand, and be in relationship with Jesus the Christ. So the legitimate *primary* content of Christian teaching is not a text or a creed, but a person—Jesus Christ—and the believer's relationship with him!

The approach. Given that the context of Christian education is a faith community, and given that the content is the person of Jesus, then the way we go about the work of teaching and learning needs to be relational. The most damaging unexamined assumption that exists in Christian teaching today is that teaching *about* God is tantamount to providing an experience *of* God; that to know *about* God is the same as *knowing* God. What commonly passes for Christian teaching often suggests that teaching about what the Bible says about Jesus is tantamount to introducing people to Jesus on a personal level.

Author Henri J. M. Nouwen correctly argues that Christian education is not primarily ministry because of its content, but because of the nature of the education process itself. He warns that "perhaps we have paid too much attention to the content of teaching without realizing that the teaching *relationship* is the most important factor in the ministry of teaching."[5] In dialogical learning, the most meaningful interaction with the greatest potential for learning the Christian faith and for growth in Christ takes place between persons in small groups that are characterized by love, trust, honesty, and mutual encouragement. These are conditions for communication of faith. Dialogical learning is relationship, and it exemplifies the conviction that Christian education must use Christian principles if it is to be effective.

Teaching as relationship has radical implications for the group leader. First, content is internal rather than external, for the teacher and group members can only communicate as much Christianity as they have assimilated. Being a teacher for the spiritual formation of the learners in the group involves not learning techniques, but "paying the price of letting God work you over, being purified by the fire of divine love, undergoing transformation from within by divine grace."[6]

Second, since relationship is the most important dynamic in Christian education and since the Holy Spirit is the *real* source of spiritual formation and growth, then any member of the community can be called upon to be a spiritual teacher. In most churches, there are many more members who can be spiritual friends to others than we give opportunity to do so through formal programs such as Sunday school. Christian education for spiritual formation will call and support all mature learners to be relational teachers. Through small groups using dialogical learning approaches, churches can free up the treasure house of spiritual gifts, wisdom, and participation in the ministry of teaching and encouragement that so many of our members crave to provide.

Third, teaching as relationship paradoxically involves both submission and mutuality. Progress in the spiritual life is enhanced when members of the community make themselves accountable to one another. Without submission, the learner cannot learn from the discernment, teachings, or counsel of others. At the same time, teaching as relationship involves a genuine mutuality between teacher and learners as well as among learners. Clergy, teachers, educators, and mentors do not have a monopoly on spiritual growth. With no privileged status for the role of teacher, it is assumed that the teacher, leader, or guide will be open and subject to change. Small study groups can facilitate mutuality of submission through the practice of covenant. (See appendix B for a sample group covenant.)

The outcome. While for traditional schooling, the outcome is mastery of content, if the content of Christian education is a *person*, then mastering content does not make sense. Since Christian education is relational, then the outcome of teaching is to be changed by that relationship, to deepen that relationship, and to *become* as a result of that relationship. Additionally, the nature of Christian faith is corporate. One is Christian by virtue of being part of the body of Christ—by being in relationship with Christ and with the other persons in one's community of faith. Therefore, another necessary outcome is to be in relationship with the persons who make up the fellowship and community known as God's church.

The methodology. Schooling often focuses on and encourages individual learning, sometimes even competitive ways of learning that pit one person's mastery, abilities, and accomplishments against those of another. Christian education, which has a person for its content, a community for its context, and being-in-relationship with others as its driving dynamic approach, cannot function within the boundaries of a schooling model. As author and educator Morton Kelsey puts it, a Christian education that is genuine must use methodologies that are Christian.[7] The more legitimate methodologies for Christian teaching, then, are reflective of those dialogical learning approaches in which Christian education happens within the context of the faith community. Schooling and Christian education diverge on two significant questions. Schooling values *what* one knows and suggests that we are saved by knowledge of content. Christian education values *who* one knows and recognizes that we are saved by that relationship. Yet it seems that despite our belief that the Christian life is about knowing Christ, we often go about teaching people as if we believe that *what* we know is more important than *who* we know!

DIALOGICAL LEARNING FACILITATES COMMUNITY

Dialogical learning provides a powerful way of harnessing the inherent collective memory of the individuals who make up the faith community in which Christian education takes place and that forms the identity of the believers. We not only learn in the church, we *are* the church. This shared collective memory consists of shared experiences and the core biblical story of faith that gives the church its identity. People need to actually speak these things to each other, to listen to themselves saying these things, and to listen to others share them.

Dialogical learning is one of the ways that people form a corporate sense of self or "group identity." In dialogical learning, people not only learn more about themselves through the process of articulating what they think and feel, but they also incorporate the things others share.

Dialogical learning facilitates the points of intersection where "my" thoughts and "your" thoughts become "our" thoughts. In genuine community, values are negotiated, but that only happens when people talk to each other honestly and openly. Dialogue also provides a safe place where people can share doubts and sincere questions about faith without fear of being criticized because it fosters the understanding that doubt is not in opposition to faith. The opposite of faith is, in fact, certitude or the assumption that one's understanding of faith is "fixed." This is an attitude that leaves no room for growth.

The purpose of dialogical learning is to allow persons to relate to each other in the context of their community of faith. As persons engage in dialogical learning, they discover truths about each other that cannot otherwise be discovered. They do not talk *at* each other; rather,

Stewardship: A Case in Point

Stewardship is about a Christian's personal, volitional response to God's call to discipleship as part of the body of Christ. As such, stewardship is first a value, second a practice (behavior), and third a concept or belief. We tend to "teach" it backward and incompletely, too often using the teaching-by-telling approach and leaving it at that. As a spiritual issue, stewardship must be addressed like every other spiritual issue, addressing the affective, volitional, and behavioral domains. The task is not to *tell* people that they need to give 10 percent of their money to the church; rather, it is to help people arrive at a conviction of value by engaging them in the dialogue of theological reflection by asking, "How are you responding to God in your stewardship of life?"

Our failure to help our members learn—really learn—stewardship has had tragic results. We have done a great disservice to our members over the years by being ineffective in addressing the stewardship dimension of discipleship (except for the annual church budget, and all evidence is that we have failed even there, since most members give only between 2.2 and 2.9 percent of their income to the church).[8] I suspect that we, the church leaders—pastors, teachers, deacons—have been irresponsible because we ourselves have not dealt with issues related to money. In many churches, a significant number of members are under an oppressive burden of debt, so much so that they are *unable* to respond in responsible stewardship to God. And I suspect they resent church leaders for it because we have been of no help in the area of financial stewardship, while, at the same time, making them feel guilty about not giving more money.

they share *with* each other on all levels that matter: ideas, feelings, and values. In that process, people begin to really know each other and, amazingly enough, they get to know themselves more deeply. The process of dialogical learning helps people understand and appreciate what other people believe and why. This process of mutual understanding yields empathy—the ability to stand in the other's place, to see things from his or her perspective, and to appreciate where he or she is coming from without necessarily agreeing. The Christian term for that is *grace!* Author and pastor Albert J. Wollen puts it this way: "When Christians get back into dialogue with each other and when there develops deep personal sharing—only then can the world be impressed with our message of reconciliation. Dialogue is essential to a true expression of the church as it seeks to reach the world around us."[9]

We have not been prophetic about challenging the values of the world that our members have embraced and the myths of materialism the world teaches. So when once or twice a year we make our pitch for money, they can't hear it, at least not theologically. Using dialogical learning in small groups is a much more effective way to bring about change in stewardship because it touches areas in people's lives that teaching-by-telling can never address. Since the issue of stewardship is not monolithic, we ought to address it in the same way we address issues about faith development and discipleship: by taking into account developmental life stages and cycles. Different epochs in life require different messages about stewardship of life. For example, midlife calls for a stewardship of generativity (learning to face the limitation of means and beginning to invest in the next generation—in effect, learning how to give one's life away). Adolescents and young adults, on the other hand, are in a life stage that appropriately includes acquiring and building. And how unfair and nonsensical are messages about stewardship of money to young children, who have no money and no cognitive concept of percentages or proportional giving? I think we confuse people and make them feel uselessly guilty when we send the message that, regardless of their life stage, their family life cycle stage, and their particular life situation, they are supposed to function and respond like "everyone else." Further, we rarely give the opportunity for learning through dialogue that leads to application. Stewardship is as much a value and a choice as it is a concept and a practice. Unless we address all four domains, our members will never "learn" stewardship.

DIALOGICAL LEARNING FACILITATES THEOLOGICAL REFLECTION

One very valuable by-product of dialogical learning in small groups is that people learn how to "think theologically." The ability of a church's members to practice theological reflection is one of a church's most valuable resources. I suspect that most of the misguided, costly, and tragic decisions made in church, from business meetings to educational programming, could be averted if the members of the church were able to think theologically about matters. People also need to think theologically about all aspects of their lives: their relationships, their stewardship, their jobs and vocations, and their church. And the only way they learn how to think theologically is to practice thinking theologically. To put the matter simply, Christians need to be able to answer the question, "What is the theology that informs our practices, beliefs, attitudes, values, decisions, and behaviors?"

The tragedy is that most Christians do not even ask the question. I suspect that for most of our church members, the concerns and decisions of their lives are informed by every source (financial, personal taste, predilections, trends, fads, commercialism, materialism, peer pressure, culture) other than the theological. If members of the Christian church have any hope of living like Christians, they need to develop a distinctly Christian identity and a Christian worldview. One minister friend of mine often bemoans the fact that, looking at the homes in which his members live, he can discern no difference in lifestyle between those families and the other families on the block. This begs the question: What difference does it make that you call yourself a Christian?

People practice theological reflection by talking about their life experiences. It is through narrative, sharing their life stories, that people do the work of making meaning. And it is through dialogical learning that people can create that narrative, sharing and exploring with others how the Bible and Christian truths intersect with their life experiences. This powerful process of theological reflection takes place in the context of one's faith community, the church, which provides correctives, such as biblical metaphors, to help people think theologically. Biblical metaphors and the stories that carry them help church members in their development of a Christian worldview. In fact, that's what those stories and metaphors are there for! In the next chapter, we will examine the essential elements of dialogical learning in the small group context and the role of the teacher-facilitator.

CHAPTER 3

Understanding and Using Group Dynamics

In this chapter we will examine what makes a small group work as it does. The focus of this chapter is on helping you, the group leader, to understand the basic dynamics of a small group, which include "group math," group roles, and group formation. More important, this chapter aims at helping you know how best to use small group dynamics to aid the group in becoming an effective learning environment.

Small groups are varied and complex. A small group that meets for study meets to learn, to gain knowledge, to get insight, and to understand its focus of study, whether it is the Bible, a topic, or a book. This kind of group needs to meet from an hour to 90 minutes to engage in dialogical learning. During that time, myriad interrelated and interrelational group dynamics are at play. Some of these dynamics facilitate learning and dialogue, while others may impede learning.

The Essential Elements of Dialogical Learning

For dialogical learning to be effective in a small group, four essential elements and conditions must exist: *trust, unity, intentional objectives*, and *an effective facilitator*. Let's examine how each of these essential elements helps make dialogical learning possible in a small group.

Trust. For dialogical learning to happen, the members must trust one another. Trust is what makes honest sharing possible. When trust is achieved in the group, things happen that allow members to achieve meaningful learning through dialogue. Members are able to respond to the challenge to suspend their assumptions and prejudices when approaching a topic or Bible passage. This facilitates meaningful learning, because no one in the group is out to "win" or feels the need to "be right" about the matter under exploration. When group members understand that dialogical learning is a process of discovery, they may confirm what they believe and value or they may challenge currently held beliefs. Trust is what makes group members willing to risk the challenge of change, which is essential because learning is change.

One important group dynamic in dialogical learning is the ability to suspend one's assumptions and opinions until one has heard the other person's opinions. Group members must learn to listen to one another in trust and suspend judgment until later in the learning experience when judgment is called for. Only when members feel that they can trust the group will they feel free to be honest about their feelings and share what they believe. That is, only when trust exists will learners be willing to be vulnerable for the sake of learning. Dialogical learning, then, requires that the group provide a safe space for people to share freely without fear of being judged or silenced.

Unity. Group unity occurs when all members see themselves as co-learners in the learning process. There are no experts in the Christian life. No one has mastered discipleship or achieved the status of "über disciple." The person who has been a "lifelong Christian" has as much to learn as the recent convert. In a dialogical learning group, all members accept that they are participant colleagues and fellow travelers on the journey of growth in the Christian life. Therefore, even the group leader becomes a co-learner in the group. He or she understands that the role of teaching is not to be the resident expert but, rather, a facilitator for learning.

Intentional objectives. The dialogical learning process must have intent—that is, there must be a clear reason why the group meets and studies. Intent requires the facilitator, often with the group's help, to identify appropriate learning objectives to frame the learning experience. The intent of dialogical learning is to provide a structured, intentional process that leads to insights and deep understanding and ultimately to application in the life of the learner. The goal of each learning experience is to foster the application of Christian truth in the lives of the participants.

An effective group facilitator. Because dialogical learning has a particular intent and methodology, the role of group facilitator becomes critical. For one thing, most people have had little experience with this kind of discovery approach to dialogical learning. New members to the group often want to engage in "discussion" and think that they need to advocate or defend a "right" opinion or interpretation. They often have trouble getting comfortable with the fact that the experience is more about challenging assumptions in order to facilitate growth than it is about agreement or consensus or affirmation of belief. The skilled group facilitator is indispensable in helping the group create and maintain the kind of environment that allows the group members to speak honestly while risking being challenged in a way that is not threatening. "Unlearning" something is one the most difficult things for people to do. The reason for this is that we tend to have an emotional investment in what we believe—even if it is wrong. The most common initial response to having a belief or assumption challenged is to defend it. A facilitator monitors group process to create the space not only for sharing with one another, but also for listening to one another. That is important, because to engage in the work of dialogical learning, the learner needs to first feel that he or she is being heard.[1]

For dialogical learning to take place, the teacher of the small study group will need to make a shift in his or her understanding of the role of "teacher." No longer is the teacher in the role of "instructor"; rather, the teacher now functions as a "facilitator" of learning. This can be a challenge for many teachers who have become comfortable with the teaching-by-telling method or who have a personal need to be the "expert" in the room or the "sage on the stage." This kind of shift in roles may require giving up some long-held assumptions about what "teaching" is supposed to be. It will require a step in faith that the Spirit of God is the real teacher when two or more are gathered in Jesus' name. This kind of shift means giving up control in order to allow the Spirit to move in the lives of the learners. And it requires trusting that the learners in the group can and will be teachers to one another. Any obstacles can be overcome if the small study group teacher is willing to make a commitment to becoming an *effective* group leader. Here is the

> ## The Teaching Role in Dialogical Learning
>
> - I will structure my teaching around students as active participants.
>
> - I will shift my position from "resident expert" to learning process facilitator.
>
> - I will shift the primary approach from telling to discovering and guiding.
>
> - I will create an environment of trust, openness, and challenge.
>
> - I will monitor the learning process to ensure direction and intentional outcomes in learning.
>
> - I will offer dialogical questions for participants and encourage them to raise their own questions.

challenge: the small group leader can be an obstacle to learning or a facilitator of learning. Which do you want to be? If you are able to make these shifts in your teaching role, you will unleash the power of dialogical learning and will facilitate meaningful learning for your group members. And meaningful learning will enable transformation-application of Bible or theological truths in the lives of your learners.

How Groups Form

Groups are "living" entities that take on lives of their own. You have probably experienced this yourself if you are in a position to visit different classes or groups. Each group or class seems to have its own "personality," and anyone entering that group or class as a new member tends to adapt to that corporate personality. How much this phenomenon is dependent on the group leader or teacher is hard to determine. I give certain courses and workshops over and over again—same material, same methods, same pace, same stories and illustrations, yet every time I offer a particular course or workshop with a different group of people, they form a "personality" of their own, which makes for a totally different experience—despite the fact the material hasn't changed and the teacher hasn't changed.

Like all living things, groups are birthed, go through a process of development, and run the course of their life cycle. Being able to recognize the life cycle of your small group can help you interpret what your group is going through and will help you guide it along through its natural developmental transitions. Let's examine the four phases of group development: (1) invitation and orientation, (2) norming and forming, (3) trust and differentiation, and (4) closure and dissolution.

1. Invitation and orientation phase. At some point in time, someone decides that a small group is needed. The next logical step, then, is to extend invitations to persons to become part of the new group. People join groups for many reasons. As I like to remind my students, "Never question other people's motives." The bottom line is that a person will choose to join a group when he or she perceives that the group will meet a personal need.[2] The personal need that a person may want a small group to meet often is not the same as the overtly stated purpose of the group; therefore, it is not uncommon for persons to drop out in this early stage of group formation. Participant loss need not be seen as a failure if it is a result of the group being clear about its purpose so that some participants recognize that the group is not for them. Not every group is for everybody, and there's nothing wrong with that.

Effective groups have clearly defined purposes and clear parameters about who is invited to join. For example, when starting a new group for parents, it is helpful to overtly state a criterion, such as "for parents whose oldest child at home is ten years old or younger."

Because a dialogical learning group is one that has *a structured, intentional process that leads to insights and deep understanding and,*

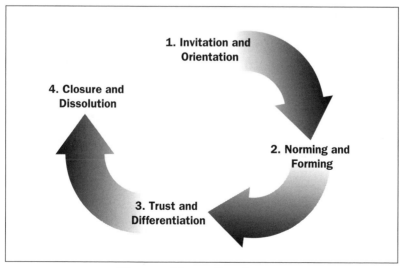

Phases of Group Development

ultimately, application in the life of the learner, the orientation phase is very important. The small group teacher-facilitator must invest intentional time and attention in this orientation stage. Educator and writer Roberta Hestenes speaks to the danger of not giving this stage its due attention:

> Simply to invite people to join a "Christian small group" or a "Bible study group" does not tell them clearly what they are joining and what obligations are involved. This general invitation does not adequately express what the group does or means to accomplish specifically. If you invite someone to a Bible study group, for example, it is possible that they will anticipate sitting in a class where a teacher provides information and where they are merely listeners rather than actively involved in the discussion and participating in what's going on.[3]

2. Norming and forming phase. Once the group has passed the invitation and orientation phase, it settles into the messy stage of norming and forming. This is where group members rub up against one another, test limits, stake out positions and territory, negotiate friendships—even vie for the seating arrangement! This stage sometimes involves misunderstanding, conflict, and fights for control. This is logically so because the group has yet to establish its corporate norms and rules, formal and informal. An effective small group leader will understand that this is a normal and necessary part of group development and will allow appropriate discomfort in the group. Often, the worst thing the leader can do is try to solve all of the emerging frustrations or try to ease the group's anxiety too quickly. There is great value in letting group participants solve these issues for themselves, because *this is how they become a group.*

There are, however, some things the group leader can address. Good groups don't "just happen." Good groups are made, and it is the responsibility of the group leader to help that take place. This is especially true for dialogical learning small groups. For example, this is the stage when the group leader can guide the group members through a group covenant. Creating or agreeing to a group covenant is a large part of what norming and forming are all about. Intentionally investing in a covenanting process with the group will go a long way toward navigating the sometimes turbulent waters of the norming and forming stage. When group members work through the process of defining

and agreeing to a group covenant, they in effect help establish and articulate the group norms.[4]

Additionally, group members must be trained in how to be participants who help facilitate dialogical learning. The group members will
learn some of this along the way, but some of this cannot be left to
chance.[5] The good news is that it does not take groups long to work
through the often messy norming and forming stage. In fact, if groups
are to survive, they need to work through this stage quickly! Otherwise,
early dissolution is likely. A positive but firm group leader will be an
asset and resource to the group as members work through this phase.

3. Trust and differentiation phase. Having come through the messi-
ness of working out its identity and norms, the group arrives at a more
settled phase where trust can begin to take hold. This stage is characterized by a sense of cohesiveness. The group as a whole has developed to
the point where its members are comfortable enough with each other to
express divergent views and opinions. Group members are beginning to
"be themselves" in the group—becoming more transparent and honest
because they feel they really "belong" to the group. The group as a
whole develops a "personality," or group identity. Group members are
able to talk about "us" and "we" when referring to the group, and outsiders can often be overheard talking about "that group."

Within the group, members differentiate themselves by taking on
roles and functions. The intriguing part about small group dynamics is
that these roles and functions seem to be universal to groups, despite
variables like personality and temperament. The ways these roles come
about seem to be dictated more by the synergy of group dynamics than
individual preferences or factors. In fact, individual group roles may be
more about the functioning of the group than about the functioning of
the individuals that make up the group. This is another powerful example that groups take on a life of their own. We will examine individual
group roles in more detail.

Paradoxically, the dialogical learning approach may facilitate a
greater amount of confrontation than in the previous phase of group
development, but in this stage it is done with relative ease and in a
nonthreatening manner. Remember that dialogical learning includes
helping people be open to the kind of challenge that leads to growth—
speaking the truth in love, as Paul says (Ephesians 4:15). At this stage
members feel free to share both positive and negative feedback with

each other. This is a sign that the members of the group have taken to heart their roles of being teachers and learners together. In other words, they have taken responsibility for their learning!

4. Closure and dissolution phase. All good things must come to an end, the saying goes, and this holds true for groups. At this stage the group members tend to look for direction from the group leader about how to engage in a closure process. This is a time of reflection, sharing, and saying good-bye to the group. Grieving is allowed. One important step may be to help the members express expectations, or their struggle, about how to relate to the other members of the group as individuals after the group is no longer there to bind them together.

The dissolution phase can include a recommitment component. For example, the group members may choose to continue as a small group for another period of time. In this case, some renegotiation is appropriate and can include anything from what the group will study next to how it will do certain things differently. This is a good time to give permission for some persons to leave the group and also to extend invitations to new members to join.

GROUP MATH

One of the most interesting dynamics of small groups is how the number of participants who make up the group affect interaction and dialogue and, therefore, how that factor impacts learning. It may be wrong to think about the "right" number of participants who make up a good small group. The better question may be, "What is the best number of participants in this group for what I want to accomplish?" However, without a doubt, this will always be true: the larger the group, the less opportunity there is for participation and discussion, sharing, and dialogue. As the size of the group increases, more and more members participate less and less. The result is that a few members tend to dominate the discussion more as more group members participate less.[6]

Small study groups can vary from three persons to twenty-five persons. Each combination of participants in the group impacts the small group dynamics in different ways. The chart "Group Math" shows which small group size is best suited for which learning task. If your small group is too large to be effective in accomplishing a certain task, then you can decide to form smaller learning groupings for the purpose of your learning outcome.

Group Math

Small Group Size	Good for:
Dyad (2 persons)	intimate sharing and efficient processing of simple concepts or personal experience that does not need to be shared with the larger group as a whole.
Triad (3 persons)	discussion and dialogue, but has drawbacks and limitations. For example a "two-against-one" dynamic might develop, or two dominant members might shut out a passive member.
4 persons	discussion questions and dialogue. Can effectively handle up to five dialogical questions in an allotted time period of at least 40 minutes.
5 persons	processing discussion questions and dialogue. Can effectively handle three to four dialogical questions in an allotted time of at least 45 minutes.
9 persons	for a problem-solving task. This size group will come up with just about every possible solution to a problem without getting stuck.
15 persons	optimum small group. This size group can remain intimate and interactive with enough space and time and with a good teacher-facilitator, and can also form smaller units for more effective discussion followed by debriefing.
18 persons	a traditional class in which the teacher-leader facilitates dialogical learning by consistently forming smaller units for learning. Whole group dialogical discussion may still be possible with a highly skilled leader.
25 persons	classroom instruction, maximum size for a "small group." A good teacher-facilitator will need to work intentionally and consistently to overcome the logistics of this larger group. Dialogical learning becomes difficult without consistently regrouping into smaller discussion groups. Often the best strategy is to form two smaller permanent groups out of the one.

THE ROLES PEOPLE PLAY

As mentioned above, sometime during the trust and differentiation phase, something very interesting, and necessary, happens in the group. The individual members of the group take on specific individual group roles and functions. This comes about in the give-and-take of group formation. Some persons volunteer for certain roles, others take them on by default, and others appear to be assigned their roles. Regardless of the individual who gets the group role, the roles themselves serve a function for the group as a whole. It is not uncommon to observe that when one member of the group is absent or leaves the group, another member takes on that person's vacated role or function because the role has more to do with the group dynamic than with the particular individual who holds that role.

I am keenly aware of how I function in the different groups to which I belong. In some of them, I somehow play roles that are contrary to my normal temperament. Yet I have no problem functioning in that uncharacteristic (for me) role within *that* group. How exactly that came to be remains a mystery to me—except I know enough to accept that this is how groups work.

We can divide the various individual group roles that people take into the three broad categories of group task function roles, group maintenance roles, and unhealthy group roles. These individual roles have been identified, named, and described in many ways over the years.

Group Task Function Roles

Group task function roles are related to the tasks which the group is undertaking, like engaging in dialogue, solving a problem, engaging in a learning activity, or making a decision. Persons who take on these roles facilitate and coordinate group process in selecting and defining a problem and working toward the solution to the problem. In the dialogical learning process, these roles serve the group well in keeping the group dialogue at a level of high quality and focused on its purpose.

The Director enjoys "taking charge" in ways that help the group get started, move along, or get unstuck, and can be very task-oriented. ("Hey folks, let's get started, please. We want to use as much time as we can on good discussion!" Or, "Would everyone please grab a Bible and stack it here before you leave. And please clean up any coffee cups in your area. We want to leave the room clean.")

The Elaborator helps the group members develop concepts more fully, challenges members to explain responses to questions more accurately, and checks for comprehension. ("What do you mean by that, exactly?" Or, "I'm not sure I understand what you mean. Can you give me an example?")

The Orienter familiarizes the group with new ideas or orients new members to the group. (To a new member: "Bob is our resident expert on the matter; he can talk forever on the subject!")

The Summarizer summarizes what has occurred, points out departures from agreed-upon goals, and brings the group back to the central issues. ("So, are we all agreed on this point? I'd like to get clear on where we stand before we move on.")

The Evaluator subjects the accomplishments of the group to standards and questions the practicality, logic, and facts of arguments. ("That's an interesting point, but is that what the text really says?" Or, "That sounds like 'either-or' thinking. Aren't there any other options than just those two?")

Group Maintenance Roles

The roles under the category of group maintenance function to help the group members work as a group. They alter, redirect, or maintain the group's normal ways of working. The actions associated with these roles serve to strengthen and preserve the group norms.

The Administrator solves or addresses administrative problems but does not address interpersonal or process problems within the group. ("We're passing around a sheet. Please put your name and e-mail address on the list so we can contact everyone in case we need to change our meeting date." Or, "Please remember to put some money in the coffee till if you have a cup or eat some cookies. We don't want complaints from our hosts.")

The Harmonizer serves to mediate differences among members and attempts to reconcile disagreement and relieve tensions in conflict situations. ("It's all right to challenge an opinion, but I don't think it's helpful to question motives. Don't you agree?" Or, "Mary, I don't think Bob was criticizing you. Bob, can you say that in a different way so Mary can better understand what you're saying?")

The Compromiser or Mediator proposes possible solutions or approaches that will meet most needs. ("Okay, how about this? How about we just agree that we can't solve this issue? Can we move on to the second point?" Or, "Well, I don't fully agree with this decision personally, but I'll go along with it as a group member.")

The Encourager encourages others to continue to be involved. ("Susan, I've noticed that you've really been working hard to stay in there even though it seems you feel the group is sometimes at a different place than you are. I really admire that!")

The Cheerleader has praise for everything and everyone. ("I just want to say that this is the best study group I've ever been a part of!" Or, "Sam, you always seem to say the right things at the right time. Thanks for that!")

The Gatekeeper keeps communication channels open by encouraging or facilitating the participation of quiet members or by proposing regulation of the flow of communication. ("Sarah, you've been kind of quiet today. What do you think about all this?" Or, "I know that John has had experience with this sort of situation. He may have a different perspective on it than what we've been hearing so far." Or, "I really think we need to hear from each person in the group on this issue. Let's go around the room and check where each of us is on this matter.")

Unhealthy Group Roles

Particular persons in a group take on group task functioning and group maintenance roles on a more or less permanent basis. This is why when a new person comes into a group and finds that someone already occupies a "favorite" role and is serving the group well in that capacity, he or she often takes on a different role, even though that role is a new (even unnatural) one. The roles that fall under the category of unhealthy group roles, however, may not be associated with a single person. Often these roles and functions can fluctuate from discussion to discussion or from session to session.

So while the following roles are easily identifiable and distinct, the group leader will need to understand that none may define one person in the group permanently or completely. People are not automatons; their feelings, states of mind, and attitudes change with the circumstances. Therefore, it is more helpful to identify and deal with the unhealthy group roles one person may manifest as a product of the immediate group process than to label or identify one particular person with that unhealthy role.

However, when these unhealthy roles do get patterned and become a characteristic of one person in particular, it often spells trouble and frustration for both the group as a whole and for the group leader. When these roles become patterned in the group process and become predictable in the learning experience, dialogical learning will be blocked at some level or at some point. It may not be an overstatement to say that more often than not, when these unhealthy functions pop up, they have less to do with the group itself and more to do with something that is going on in the life of the participant manifesting the unhealthy role. Here are some of the most common unhealthy group roles that exist in the small group context.

The Blocker may come across as negative and stubborn, resisting, disagreeing, and opposing without reason. Blocking actions interfere with the learning progress of the group by intentionally deviating from the subject of discussion, citing personal experiences unrelated to the problem, rejecting ideas without consideration, or arguing excessively. The group facilitator will do well to take the focus off the blocker, bypass blocking comments, and move the group dialogue along.

The Dominator tries to assert herself or himself by attempting to manipulate members of the group. This group member may want to take control of the discussion or to be perceived as "boss" or leader in the group. Weak groups tend to have great difficulty controlling a dominator, so often the group leader must step in and reassert leadership to help the group regulate this behavior.

The Resister digs in his or her heels and refuses to be put into a position of having to commit to anything. The person exhibiting this attitude can interfere with the goal of being challenged and changed in order to grow, but resistance is also often a sign of the first step toward change. The key here is to facilitate ways for the group to get past the resistance.

The Critic becomes critical of everything and everyone, often to gain status. The Critic can be an aggressor whose comments may feel or sound like attacks. In these cases, it is often helpful for the group leader to take the person aside for some personal coaching, since frequently the Critic is unaware of how he or she comes across. The group facilitator can coach the person on how to put forth opinions and make comments without shutting down dialogue or sounding like an attack.

The Follower goes along with anything. At worst the person in this role exhibits passive-aggressive behaviors, such as withdrawing, acting indifferently or passively, resorting to excessive formality, daydreaming, doodling, whispering to others, and wandering from the subject. The person taking on this role is a challenge in several ways. First, this person fails to contribute to the group and so denies the other group members of the resources he or she can provide. Second, the passive-aggressive follower is resistant to change and challenge and therefore resists growth. This may be one of the most difficult roles to address, because the more the leader pushes, the more the person may retreat. Sometimes you can change the function of a follower by putting him or her in a position in which he or she must lead.

The Celebrity seeks recognition and can be distractive to the group because he or she works in various ways to call attention to himself or herself through boasting, unusual acts, or reporting of personal accomplishments. Obviously, this is a needy posture, but sometimes the most helpful way to handle a celebrity is simply to ignore him or her.

The Fighter is similar to the Dominator, though more aggressive in his or her actions. The Fighter often works for status by criticizing or blaming others, showing hostility against the group or an individual, or deflating the ego or status of others. While the Dominator just wants his or her due, the Fighter is invasive. The mistake group leaders and group members make when dealing with fighters is trying to "reason" with them. There are in fact only two ways to deal with a fighter: (1) don't fight back (it takes two to tango), or (2) fight back and win (or if you don't win, at least you'll both come away bloody but good friends).

The Competitor is always vying with others to produce the best ideas, to talk the most, to play the most roles, or to gain the leader's favor. This person impedes collaborative learning and can move toward a domineering role. Sometimes a simple reminder from the group facilitator that "this is not a contest," will help regulate the competitor. Because the dialogical learning approach in the small group is so different from what many people have experienced, they often have trouble letting go of assumptions that learning involves competition—getting a better grade, getting the teacher's attention, finishing first, or being the "best in class."

The Needy wants recognition of his or her feelings and personal needs by seeking attention through loud or excessive talking, extreme ideas, or unusual behavior. Needy persons often want the group to take care of them. Sadly, the needy posture does not lead to growth or maturity. It may well be that the needy group member will be the one who faces the most challenge and discomfort through the dialogical learning approach, which aims at helping people take responsibility for their own learning. The worst thing a group can do for the person who adopts this role is to give in to the urge to take care of the person.

The Whiner tends to engage in special pleading for personal concerns or to seek sympathy. Whiners often ask for dispensation for their tardiness, lack of follow-up, and lack of contributing to the welfare of the group. They often introduce suggestions related to personal concerns or predilections. They also engage in lobbying, inappropriate self-confessing, asking advice of the group or using the group as a sounding board, and sometimes, expressing inappropriate personal feelings or points of view. The whiner can be very distractive and, if this is a patterned personal role, very destructive of the group learning process.

One of the hardest, but often necessary, steps a group may need to take for the sake of the group is to "uninvite" a Whiner. Most groups tend to carry the Whiner for longer than they should, causing the group to spend time regrouping before they can move on to the work at hand. The Whiner may have genuine needs that he or she is seeking, inappropriately, to alleviate through the group. It is best to help this person find the help he or she needs outside of the study group context.

The Joker in a small group study setting can be disruptive. I am not talking here about the person who provides levity to reduce tension in the group, but about the person akin to "the class clown" whose clowning, joking, mimicking, and lack of seriousness disrupts the work of the group. Often the Joker has no ill intent; he or she just (1) doesn't know when to stop joking and get down to business or (2) wants to avoid the serious work of learning, study, and growing. Staying in a joking state of mind does not facilitate introspection, pensiveness, or reflection, things necessary for the dialogical learning process.

Understanding basic group dynamics can help the group facilitator guide the dialogical learning process more effectively. In fact, training the group members themselves in how groups work can empower them to understand what is happening when they feel stuck and know what to do to be able to self-regulate and get back on track. As a group leader, you will find it very helpful to identify what individual group members are doing to both help and hinder the dialogical learning process through the group roles they adopt. This can go a long way in helping you not to "personalize" the group roles persons take on, especially the unhealthy ones. When you are able to identify these roles and their functions, you can better respond in ways that are useful to the group and the individual members that make up the group.

In the next chapter we will examine how to develop and use dialogical learning questions for the small group study process. The skill of asking questions—asking the right questions in the right way—is one of the most important skills a group leader needs to learn to ensure effectiveness in the small group learning process.

CHAPTER 4

Developing
Dialogical Questions

Does the following scenario sound familiar to you?

The group members are settling in. The teacher walks in and, after taking a few minutes to get ready, starts the class by saying, "Good morning! I hope you are all ready for today's lesson; it's a really good one!" After reading the Bible text of the day, the teacher begins the lesson by asking, "Do you think God answers prayers today in the same way he did in Bible times, even though none of us prays like they did back then? (Well, maybe you do; I don't know. Ha, ha.) If people today prayed like they did in Bible times, could it make any difference in how God responds?" Pause. Four seconds of silence, then the teacher says, "Let me put it another way. On the evidence we have, do miracles still happen today, and does God still answer prayers? Did God listen better and respond in Bible times? Were those times different for Christians?" Pause. Another three seconds of silence, and the teacher says, "Didn't anybody read the Bible passage for this week?"

If you happened to be a member of that study group, you would have a few questions of your own, such as, "What is she asking? Which question does she want me to answer? Is she asking about prayer or about miracles? What is this lesson about anyway?" But, more than

43

likely, you would have stopped listening because your brain tuned out, and as a result, you would settle in for an hour during which you did not expect to learn anything.

Effective dialogical questions are at the heart of the dialogical learning approach to the small study group. This chapter will help you understand how to write and use questions that facilitate dialogical learning. We will examine the different types of questions that are useful for the dialogical process. Learning how to write and use effective dialogical questions will help you overcome the null-expectancy factor of your group members and move them toward meaningful learning.

The purpose of dialogical questions is, simply, to facilitate the dialogical learning experience, which, as you will recall, is *a structured, intentional process that leads to insights and deep understanding and, ultimately, application in the life of the learner.* The three operative and interrelated terms in this definition are *insights, understanding,* and *application.* Insight has to do with understanding the inner nature of things, but specific to dialogical learning, insight is about understanding the inner nature of oneself (the learner) and one's relationship with God and others. Understanding has to do with knowing what you know and why it is so. And application is about being able to use what you know in a variety of contexts and situations.[1]

The dialogical approach to small group study is aimed at helping learners achieve meaningful learning. We do this by facilitating a process through which group members help each other learn by sharing ideas, feelings, and experiences while they do the work of theological reflection. Theological reflection is simply thinking deeply about our experience of life—its events and relationships—through a biblical and theological framework. It is this process of working through critical questions of concern in the context of group relationship that makes this approach so powerful and potentially transformative in the lives of participants.

The importance of providing good questions for this process cannot be overstated. In fact, we can say that the extent to which the group facilitator provides effective dialogical questions for discussion is the extent to which meaningful learning will likely happen. Asking good questions, then, may be the single most important skill a good group leader can possess. To develop effective dialogical questions, the group leader must give attention to three things: (1) the three *categories* of questions, (2) the *types* of questions within each category, and (3) the *method* of asking questions.

The Categories and Types of Dialogical Questions

The three aims of dialogical learning, which are *acquiring insight, achieving understanding,* and *applying truth or knowledge,* give us the following three distinct but interrelated categories of questions:

Insight. Insight means to understand the inner nature of oneself and of one's relationship with God and others. Questions of insight help the learners uncover knowledge of their inner selves and of their relationships.

Understanding. Understanding means to know what you know and why it is so and also uncovers what you do not know. Questions of understanding help learners critically know what they know (concepts, facts, prejudices) and why it is so. Questions of understanding also help learners uncover what they do not know.

Application. Application means to use what you know in a variety of contexts and situations. Questions of application help learners use what they know in their various life situations and contexts.

The five types of dialogical questions, namely, *affective, cognitive, behavioral, volitional,* and *experiential,* fall under the three main categories of insight, understanding, and application. These types of questions reflect the domains of meaningful learning (affective, cognitive, behavioral, and vocational) that we discussed in chapter 2, as well as the very important dimension of the learner's experience. Since a forty-five-minute dialogical small group session may facilitate dealing with at most four or five questions, it is essential to craft your questions well. While you do not need to use every single *type* of question during a small group study (the types of questions that you use will depend on your learning objectives), it is important to include all of the *categories* of dialogical questions.[2]

The category of insight uses affective questions to help learners achieve insight into themselves and their relationships with God and others. Affective questions deal with *empathy, values, opinions,* and *self-awareness. Empathy* is the ability to understand the other person's point of view; to feel compassion with others and appreciate another's perspective (e.g., "How do you think you'd feel if that had happened

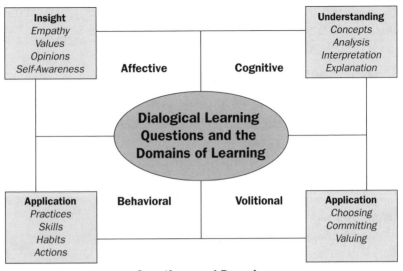

Questions and Domains

to you?" "How do you think a person would respond if. . . ?"). *Values* relates to things one holds dear and the principles to which one has committed (e.g., "Why is that important to you?" "What would make you give that up?"). *Opinions* are a person's beliefs or point of view (e.g., "What do you think about that?" "How did you arrive at that opinion?"). *Self-awareness* has to do with a sense of one's self, of one's own personality and way of being (e.g., "How are you feeling about that?" "Does that make you angry?" "Do you know why you tend to do that?" "At what times do you find yourself thinking that way?").

The category of understanding uses cognitive questions to help learners critically know what they know and why, as well as to uncover what they do not know. The four types of cognitive questions relate to *concepts, analysis, interpretation,* and *explanation. Concepts* are abstract and generic ideas about fundamental things (e.g., "In your understanding, who is a Christian and who is not?" "Can you give me your definition for the word you are using?"). *Analysis* involves the ability to separate a whole into its component parts for examination. (e.g., "Can you identify the components of that theory?" "What are the main ideas you see here?"). *Interpretation* entails explaining the meaning of something in light of past or present circumstances (e.g., "What is your theory on that?" "Can you give me an analogy or metaphor for that?" "How does that apply to today's situation?"). *Explanation* implies making something known in a way that is accurate and makes sense (e.g., "What evidence can you give to support that?" "Can you explain why that is so?" "Can you demonstrate that for us?").

The category of application uses both behavioral and volitional questions to help learners use what they know in their various life situations and contexts. Behavioral questions deal with *practices, skills, habits,* and *actions. Practices* are acts we do out of intention or commitment, often to achieve a specific end (e.g., "What is your goal for engaging in that discipline?" "How often do you practice that?"). *Skills* are special abilities acquired through practice (e.g., "How did you learn to do that?" "How would you use that skill to solve this problem?"). *Habits* are things we do as a matter of course, often uncritically, that define us (e.g., "Are you aware when you do that?" "When did you first notice that habit?"). *Actions* are behaviors done with intent, consciously or unconsciously (e.g., "Why did you do it that way?" "Do you think you could have done it differently?")

Volitional questions help learners see the practical and immediate value of what they are learning so that they will choose to apply what they have learned in everyday life. Volitional questions deal with *choosing, committing,* and *valuing. Choosing* is a volitional act whereby we make a decision of valuing one thing over another (e.g., "Why did you choose that one over the other?" "Why is that so important to you?"). *Committing* has to do with giving our devotion or dedicating ourselves to something or someone (e.g., "When did you decide to commit to that?" "What made you make that choice?"). *Valuing* has to do with the worth we ascribe to something or someone (e.g., "When did you decide that this was of worth to you?" "What does that mean to you?").

The fifth type of question, the experiential dialogical question, can almost be a category of its own. The reason you can—and should—ask experiential questions in all of the four learning domains (cognitive, affective, behavioral, and volitional) and in all three categories of dialogical questions (insight, understanding, and application) is because *connecting concepts and truths with personal experience, through the process of dialogue, is what yields meaningful learning.* Concepts, ideas, and even Bible truths that remain "outside" the learner remain meaningless to the learner. Regardless of how important those concepts or truths may be, they are not much more than trivia as far as the learner is concerned if they are not internalized. Furthermore, there can be no application of those truths unless the learner integrates them into his or her experience. The diagram below provides a visual representation of this essential and powerful fact.

People's experiences happen in three time frames: past, present, and future. Learners can remember past experiences, reflect on present experiences, and anticipate, visualize, and create future experiences. Through the process of dialogical learning, therefore, we, as group leaders, are able to connect Bible truths with the learners' experiences—past, present, and future—resulting in meaningful learning. Roberta Hestenes writes, "By inviting people to share their past, we begin to know something about the influences and experiences that have helped to make us who we are."[3] Dialogical questions related to the past solicit insights and information about the person's life history. While these kinds of questions are very effective for helping people in the group to get to know one another, asking them is also a powerful way to help people achieve insight.

Dialogical questions related to present experiences allow group members to share what is happening in their lives and thereby help them relate what they are learning to the immediacy of their concerns and needs. A puzzling and tragic phenomenon of modern church life is how little church members know about one another's lives. We do not know enough about our brothers' and sisters' daily life experiences,

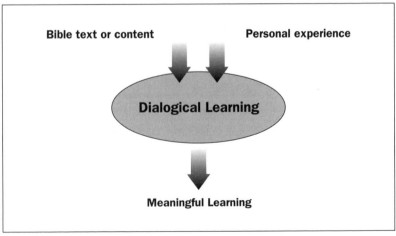

Achieving Meaningful Learning

Dialogical Questions Summary

Category	Definition	Role of Questions	Types of Questions	Domain of Learning
Insight	to understand the inner nature of oneself and of one's relationship with God and others	to help learners uncover knowledge of inner selves and of relationships	1. Affective: empathy values opinions self-awareness 2. Experiential	Affective
Understanding	to know what you know and why it is so	to help learners critically know what they know (concepts, facts, prejudices) and why it is so; and also to realize what they do not know	1. Cognitive: concepts analysis interpretation explanation 2. Experiential	Cognitive
Application	to be able to use what you know in life contexts	to help the learners use what they know in their own varied life situations and contexts	1. Behavioral: practices skills habits actions 2. Volitional: choosing committing valuing 3. Experiential	Behavioral Volitional

feelings, worries, concerns, or thoughts to even begin to minister to them in prayer or action. Furthermore, the theological reflection the members do through dialogical learning often gets them in touch with how disconnected their faith is from their own current life experiences. Asking dialogical questions of present experience helps group members become aware of the ways God is in their lives *presently.*

Dialogical questions related to future experiences can help the group members talk about their dreams, hopes, and desires, and to envision the kind of persons they want to be in response to God's call in their lives. Asking these questions can help learners define what kinds of relationships they want to have and make the decisions needed today to make that envisioned future a reality. Tapping into a learner's experiences—past, present, and future—through dialogical questions is a powerful resource for meaningful learning. It is important, then, to know how to ask questions effectively. Before moving on to "The Method of Asking Questions," take a moment to review the chart on page 49, which summarizes the preceding discussion on dialogical questions.

The Method of Asking Questions

When asking questions, we must not only pay attention to what kinds of questions we ask (the category of questions and the type of questions), but we also must be intentional about *how* we ask questions. Delivering questions in the dialogical learning small group can be done in a number of ways. During plenary, introductory, or orientation teaching time, you may use the same questioning techniques that are used in an instructional classroom setting. This can facilitate good group discussion, which is complementary to, although not equivalent to, dialogue.

Here is what you need to know: there is a way to ask a question that facilitates the learning process; asking questions any other way will inhibit the learning process in the group. The correct four-step technique to use when verbally presenting questions is as follows:

1. Ask only one question at a time and do not repeat the question.

2. Pause and wait for a response from the learner.

3. Acknowledge the response.

4. Ask the next question.

Regardless of what level or type of question you ask, you must always use this same four-step technique when asking a question.

If you do not follow step 1 (ask only one question at a time), you risk subjecting your learners to "question overload." Question overload happens when you ask two or more questions back to back without an intervening student response or when you repeat a single question without an intervening student response. Question overload confuses the learner, and when learners are confused, they stop thinking and therefore stop learning.

If you do not do step 2 (pause and wait for a response from the learner), you set your group up for a couple of unfortunate consequences. First, without the pause (no matter how long it takes), you'll likely wind up answering your own question or asking another question and engaging in question overload. If you answer your own question as a course of habit, you essentially train your group members that your questions are not *real* questions; you don't really expect them to answer because you already have the answers you want! Therefore, the learners figure out that they don't have to think about the questions they are asked in class.

The most challenging aspect of this step is that many teachers are afraid of silence. They assume that silence in response to a question means that nothing is happening. The truth is that, if the teacher has asked a good dialogical learning question, then silence is probably an indicator that something good is happening, namely, that group members are thinking about the question and preparing to respond. If this is the case with you, you need to (1) reframe your understanding of what silence means, and (2) raise your tolerance level for silence above that of your group's tolerance level for silence.

If you do not do step three (acknowledge the response), you inhibit learning in two ways. First, you in effect ignore the learner who has taken the time to think about your question and has formulated a response to it. Second, you do not clue the respondent or the rest of the group as to whether that response was appropriate, correct or incorrect (for fact-based questions), complete or incomplete, acceptable or not. Remember that you are teaching a group, and therefore your teaching actions must help the group as a whole learn together. When you acknowledge a student response, you let the learner know the quality of his or her response, and you help the rest of the group stay with the dialogue by not leaving them behind or confused.

Guidelines for Delivering Effective Dialogical Questions

Be clear. Avoid using vague words, such as *might, may, perhaps, some people, sometimes, could be, at times, maybe, often,* and *actually.* Say what you mean and mean what you say.

Ask "real" questions. Do not ask about the obvious. If something is self-evident in a Bible text, for example, don't waste time by asking about it. Don't answer your own questions.

Prepare questions carefully. Be sure your question falls within one of the three categories of insight, understanding, or application, or relates directly to one of the domains of learning (cognitive, affective, behavioral, or volitional). Minimize the number of nondialogical questions, such as procedural ("Are we ready to begin?" "Where's the sign-up sheet now?") or administrative ("Did everyone bring a Bible?" "Do we have enough chairs for everyone?") questions you ask.

Focus on one *idea or thought.* Each question you ask should be about one thing and only one thing. Keep your question structure simple. If you group questions on a handout, be sure they all relate to the topic or issue under discussion.

Ask open-ended questions. Avoid simplistic questions that can be answered with a yes or a no or an "I don't know." Dialogical questions are interesting. They solicit exploration and imaginative responses.

Respect the text or concept. Your questions should respect the Bible text you are exploring or the concept under study. Do not ask questions that beg a particular point of view. Your question should spark dialogue, not solicit a "right" answer.

Tap into the learner's life experience. Check to make sure that your questions are not too text- or content-oriented. The primary purpose of dialogical learning is to make meaningful learning and application happen by helping learners explore their life experiences and inner landscapes of thought and emotion in order to subject them to theological reflection.

Group leaders are sometimes afraid of what to do when a group member answers a question "wrong" or gives a confusing response. The first thing to remember is that a good dialogical question does not solicit a "right" or "wrong" response. Second, in the dialogical learning experience, it is more favorable to get a "wrong" answer than no answer! A group member who gives a wrong answer is at least engaged

Phrase interesting questions. The most interesting questions are those that are more complex, that challenge assumptions, and that tap into the imagination. Try starting some of your questions with "Why do you think," "What if," "If you could," "What might," "How would you reply to," or "Pretend you know" (for when you get that learner who responds with "I don't know").

Allow for silence. It is not uncommon for the dialogical learning small group to start off with silence as the learners read and/or think about questions. Trust the group members to get into it when they are ready. If you have asked good questions, silence indicates active, engaged learners.

Push for accountability. And teach the group members to do the same. Helping people learn how to engage in responsible dialogue and meaningful theological reflection takes time. People need to be trained to do it well. Therefore, when you hear half-hearted, fuzzy, uncritical Sunday school–style, or irresponsible answers or comments, don't criticize, but do push the learner toward accountability. Use follow-up questions, such as, "Where do you see that in the text?" "Is that what you really believe?" "What is your rationale for saying that?" "Can you cite a passage of Scripture or tell a Bible story that illustrates your point?" "What would happen if you pushed that argument to its logical conclusion?" "If you were in that situation, would you do the same?"

Broaden the discussion. If the class dialogue starts wandering, try rereading the questions to bring the group back into focus. Dialogical questions should be designed, however, as a starting point for the group learning experience. You can also broaden the discussion by asking things such as, "Does anyone have anything else to add?" "Are there other areas where these matters apply?" Often, the most important insights and understanding come through serendipity.

and putting forth effort! A good group facilitator can handle a wrong answer to keep the dialogue going.

On occasion it may be appropriate to ask fact-based questions to assess recall or knowledge. Often these are simple "right" or "wrong" questions. While the group leader does not need to spend a lot of time on these types of questions, it remains important to cue class members as to the correct facts. When a group member answers a fact-based question wrong, acknowledge the response (a simple "Thank you" will do), then continue the dialogue with follow-up questions to solicit the correct fact. For example, "Not exactly," or "Is there more?" or "Explain that." You can also turn to the class and ask, "Does anyone remember a different answer?" If you have set the right tone for the class, no one is likely to feel intimidated by answering a question "wrong." Dialogue is a process, and your group members can understand that. Sometimes "wrong" answers may just be that the leader has trouble understanding what the learner is trying to say. Rather than merely saying, "No, that's not right," develop a repertoire for dealing with vague or incomplete learner responses. See appendix D for specific ways to handle these kinds of learner responses.

A second common way to deliver dialogical questions in a small group setting is to provide a handout. This is the preferred method for delivering the key dialogical discussion questions for the group. Putting the questions on a handout allows the group to focus on the question rather than on the teacher-facilitator. It keeps the questions before them so they can refer back to them as needed. Further, it communicates in a symbolic way that it is the group members who are to take charge of the learning, as opposed to waiting on the teacher to direct the dialogue. Note that when you present the dialogical learning questions to the group on a handout, you do not need to follow the four-step technique for asking questions as outlined above.

You can group questions and subset questions on the handout (see samples in chapters 7 and 9), and typically, a small group of three to four persons can handle up to four good dialogical questions. The amount of time a group needs to do a good job on these three to four questions is about forty minutes. The more persons in the group, the more time is needed to process the questions. Therefore, working hard on designing the questions and determining what category and what type of questions to ask is critical. The effective small group leader will likely spend as much time in preparation of the dialogical questions as he or she will in studying background material on the subject at hand.

CHAPTER 5

Developing Learning Objectives for Dialogical Learning

We have defined dialogical learning in small groups as *a structured, intentional process that leads to insights and deep understanding and, ultimately, application in the life of the learner.* As the definition states, one important component of dialogical learning is that it is *intentional,* that is, the dialogical learning process aims at something specific. When we gather people together in a small group to engage in dialogical learning, we need to make clear the specific goals of the dialogue. In other words, dialogical learning is not a rambling conversation, nor is it an excuse to pool our ignorance or to reaffirm what we already believe. Nor is the purpose of dialogical learning to confirm our prejudices or our assumptions. Dialogical learning is intentional about bringing about change in the life of the learner through insight, understanding, and application.

One way to ensure intentional results is through the use of learning objectives that guide the preparation and presentation of the dialogical learning experience. In this chapter you will learn how to use learning objectives effectively for dialogical learning in the small group context. Specifically, you will learn to: (1) distinguish between a learner-centered objective and a teacher-centered objective, (2) recognize the four components of an effective learning objective, (3) identify the pros and cons of using learning objectives, and (4) write effective learning objectives for your small group's dialogical learning experience. (Just in case you missed it, the four items delineated in the preceding sentence are the learning objectives for this chapter. In this case, the learning objectives are not overt, but they are embedded in the paragraph. I could have made them more overt by putting them in a bullet list or by stating, "These are the four learning objectives for this chapter." Instead, I chose to play "hide and seek" with them and to give you a clue to the intent of this chapter through this parenthesis. The risk I run is that you are the kind of reader who skips parenthetical material, which may serve as a good example of why it is more effective to overtly state learning objectives up front—so that the learner does not miss them. Now, take a moment to review the learning objectives.)

Pros and Cons of Learning Objectives

Learning objectives are important because they will help you define the learning intent and goals of your dialogical learning experience. Writing effective learning objectives will also help point you toward appropriate group learning methods and will help your group members learn what you intend for them to learn (see chapter 6, "Effective Small Group Learning Methods"). Taking the time to write learning objectives will help you and your group members stay focused on making the dialogical learning experience lead to meaningful learning. In addition, when you write an effective learning objective, it will define for you and for your group members how you will know that learning is being achieved (learning equals change). While all this is true, there are some "cons" associated with learning objectives.

For one thing, it takes time to develop sound learning objectives. Effective learning objectives are often difficult to develop and require you to be rigorous in your thinking. This is because you must think through the issue of what makes for meaningful learning and must specify what your group members will do in the learning experience. Sometimes learning objectives can lead to embarrassment if your learners don't learn what you promised they would learn. Writing learning objectives can be difficult if you don't know what you want your learners to learn for certain topics. Or you may be unsure what they will *actually* learn once the dialogical learning experience gets underway. In this case, writing learning objectives can open your teaching up to scrutiny.

If you can get past the reality that writing effective learning objectives takes *hard work* (just like anything else that is worth doing well), you can appreciate their educational value. Writing and using learning objectives will make your group's dialogical learning much more effective. For one thing, learning objectives will keep you honest. Your clearly stated learning objectives will show what you intend to help your group members learn and what they are responsible for learning or achieving through their dialogue.

Second, learning objectives make it easy to evaluate how well your group members have learned what they studied and how well they have applied what they learned. When you and your group members are clear about the direction of the learning experience, it is easy to keep your group meetings on target. Stating your learning objectives early in the session lets learners know where the learning experience is going and what has to be done to get there.

Third, taking the time to write effective learning objectives makes it easier to design your group learning experience. Once you determine what you want your group members to have learned by the end of the session, you can more wisely choose the methods you need to use to get them there.

Finally, writing effective learning outcomes enables outsiders to the group (potential new members) to determine the value of the group's learning goals. Sharing your learning objectives with your group members can help you and them decide whether what you want to teach has sufficient value to qualify as "meaningful learning." This is important for adult learners especially, because, as we've learned, they are more selective about the potential "return on investment" of their time and energy.

Writing Learning Objectives

Most teachers and group leaders have a learning goal in mind before they start out teaching. And if you are a good group leader, you will help your group think through and decide what their learning goals will be. Goals are broad and general. They have to do with what the group wants to *learn about* or what they will be able to do. This is an appropriate place to start, but to achieve meaningful learning, we must be more specific about what will *actually* be learned. This is where a learning objective differs from a goal, and why it is so necessary to master the art of writing effective learning objectives. When it comes to education, being specific in our teaching processes is more effective than being fuzzy and vague. A sharply defined learning objective results in more effective learning than a notion.

Again, a goal tells us what we want learn about in general. It can be a vague idea or a vision about where we want to arrive. For example, a group may decide that it wants "to learn more about the Bible," or "to study the Gospel of John." Or a group leader may decide that she wants to help the group "learn to share more during discussions." A learning objective tells us *exactly* what it is that we will *actually* learn and how well we will learn it. So, starting with the goals in mind, a group may state its learning objective as "to understand John's depiction of Jesus' discourse in the gospel" or "to identify correctly the 'I am' sayings in the Gospel of John." The teacher who has the goal of helping group members learn to participate in discussions will do better to write a learning objective that reads, "The group members will identify their individual group roles in discussions," or "The group members will identify how well they meet the five characteristics of a good group discussion."

Three key terms you will need to know to write effective learning objectives are *behavior, terminal behavior,* and *criterion.* A *behavior* is any visible or measurable activity displayed by a learner. For example, "The student will tell a personal life story using a biblical metaphor." A *terminal behavior* is the behavior that the learner is to demonstrate after the learning experience. For example, "The student will tell a personal story using appropriate theological interpretation techniques." A *criterion* is the standard by which the terminal behavior is evaluated to determine how well learning has occurred. For example, "When telling a story, the student will use one of the five tools of theological reflection and interpretation."

Merely writing a learning objective correctly is insufficient for an effective learning experience. Learning is effective only when it is *meaningful* to the learner. For a learning objective to be meaningful, it must convey your intent and must be written from the standpoint of the learner. That is, it must communicate what the *learner* will learn or be able to do, not what you, the teacher or group leader, will do while teaching.

Second, a meaningful learning objective will exclude the greatest number of possible alternatives. The single greatest fault of most learning objectives is that they are written so broadly that they are meaningless. For example, an objective that states, "The student will learn to tell a story," is too vague to be helpful to you or to your learner. It does not communicate what kind of story the student will learn to tell, how well you expect the student to tell it, or what storytelling skills the student will learn. While you do not need to write all of the elements you will exclude (like not telling horror stories), you need to provide sufficient specificity so that the learner can read your objective and say, "Oh, I know exactly what I'm going to learn," or "I can see exactly what I will be able to do (or understand)."

To write an effective, meaningful learning objective for the dialogical learning process, you need to: (1) write it from the standpoint of the learner, (2) identify the terminal behavior, (3) describe the conditions under which the behavior should occur, and (4) specify the criteria for acceptable application. Here are some guiding questions to ask as you write your learning objectives:

- What do you want the learner to be able to do?
- What do you want the learner to be able to do at the end of the dialogical learning session?
- What do you want the learner to be able to do at the end of a unit of study?
- When and where do you want the learner to be able to do it?
- How well must the leaner be able to do it?

The terminal behavior. The terminal behavior is the most important characteristic of a useful objective. It identifies the kind of performance that will be accepted as proof that the learner has achieved the objective. The terminal behavior answers the question, "How do you know the learner has learned what you intended for him or her to learn?"

More important, however, it answers for the learner the question, "How will I know I've learned what I'm supposed to learn?" This connects with the definition for understanding, which is *to know what you know and why it is so.*

The more objectives you write, the more successful you will be in communicating your intent, and the clearer the group members will be about what they need to work toward. Effective terminal behaviors

- are detailed enough for group members to easily recognize the target behavior
- provide examples or illustrations to specify the type of terminal behaviors the learner will be expected to perform
- describe the situation in which the terminal behavior will be applied

The criterion. To provide for meaningful learning for your students, they need to know not only *what* they will learn, but *how well.* The criterion in your learning objective outlines the minimal acceptable performance level you expect of the learner—whether it's a skill, behavior, or affective or cognitive activity. The criterion allows the group members to determine the effectiveness of their learning experience by defining the level of success that must be achieved and the need to be very specific. This step may be difficult at first but will go a long way in helping you narrow the scope of application. "To love the world and preach the gospel to the ends of the earth," for example, is too broad to be effective and so global that it is meaningless, but "To share next week with my neighbor how my faith helped me be a better parent" is specific enough to be both achievable and measurable, and because it connects with the learner's experience, it is meaningful.

The matter of writing meaningful learning objectives can be confusing and complex. If this is the first time you have read about learning objectives, you may feel like skipping this whole thing and pressing on to teach as you always do, thinking, "Hey, I'll just trust the process. People seem to enjoy learning without all this 'rigid' learning objectives stuff." I challenge you to resist that urge. The craft of teaching is not easy to do well, but when done well, it is powerfully effective. Conversely, when it is not done well, it can lead to unfortunate results, such as creating or perpetuating the deadly null-expectancy factor. Furthermore, teaching is a high calling—so step up to the challenge of being the best small group leader you can be. Your students deserve it, and you owe it to the One who called you and equipped you to carry out this ministry. So, hang in there, and let's take a moment to review what we have learned about using learning objectives for effective dialogical learning.

- Definition: A learning objective is a statement that describes your educational intent, has three components (behavior, terminal behavior, and criterion), and is written from the standpoint of the learner.

- To write a learning objective, you need to identify and name the learning to be achieved (cognitive, behavioral, or affective), define the important conditions under which the learning is to be applied, and define the criterion of acceptable application.

See, that wasn't so hard, was it? But we can make it even easier. Below is a simple checklist to use in assessing dialogical learning objectives. Use this checklist whenever you write your own learning objectives (and you can use it to test how well other people's learning objectives are written!).

Learning Objectives Checklist

☐ Is the learning objective written from the standpoint of the learner?

☐ Is the terminal learning behavior specified?

☐ Are the conditions under which the behavior should be applied specified?

☐ Are the criteria of acceptable application specified?

☐ Can your group members understand the full intent of the objective?

Creating Objectives for Dialogical Learning

When writing learning objectives specific to the dialogical learning approach in small groups, allow yourself to be informed by the three levels of dialogical questions as discussed in chapter 4. These three basic levels for meaningful learning—insight, understanding, and application—will guide you in writing the terminal learning behavior.

The Three Levels of Dialogical Learning Objectives

Insight means to understand the inner nature of oneself and of one's relationship with God and others.	**Objectives** help the learners uncover knowledge of their inner selves and of their relationships.	**Example:** "The learner will be able to share his or her insight into how the concept of love applies to family relationships."
Understanding means to know what you know and why it is so, and also means uncovering what you do not know.	**Objectives** help the learners critically know what they know (concepts, facts, prejudices) and also come to see what they do not know.	**Example:** "The group members will be able to understand how (the meaning of) the Bible text relates to today's culture of materialism."
Application means to be able to use what you know in a variety of contexts and situations.	**Objectives** help the learners use what they know in their various life situations and contexts.	**Example:** "The group members will apply the Bible truth by identifying two specific ways they will demonstrate mercy in their work relationships."

Note: Use the Learning Objectives Checklist above to assess whether or not these sample learning objectives meet the criteria for an effective learning objective.

As you create objectives for dialogical learning, it is important to do the following:

1. Brainstorm. List the key principles, basic concepts, critical rules, and major associated facts that make up the general focus of the study. List as many as you can think of that fall within a reasonable range of difficulty for the level of learning you want your learners to achieve.

2. Define the cutoff point. Consider how deeply you can reasonably go into the subject given the amount of time dialogical learning requires. One good way to approach this point is to plan by identifying "the one thing" that is most essential. That is, if you had time to teach only one critical point, what would it be?

3. Start with the group members' current level of knowledge. Consider how familiar participants are with the material. What principles, concepts, procedures, and facts do you feel confident in assuming they already know? If you are able to answer this, even on the basis of an educated guess, you can define the starting point for the concepts or truths you hope to present. Be careful, however, because underestimating the appropriate starting point may bog down the group members in material they already know; but overestimating it may lose them.

4. Narrow the application intent. In dialogical learning, less is more, and narrower is better than broad. Think realistically about the application and the criterion for application that you will ask of the group members. These should be narrow and definite enough to be achievable. Learning is not an efficient activity. People can learn only one thing at a time, the brain can process only so much information at one time (and that amount is *very* small), and unless the learner's brain can understand what it is learning and can make an instant connection to what it already knows, it tends to stop paying attention. In the Christian life, often the best we can do is to work on learning one life-changing truth at a time. Make your objectives "small," but meaningful so that your group members can actually do what you want them to be able to do and learn what they actually need to learn.

5. Stick to what is meaningful. Remember that what you are trying to help the group members achieve is meaningful learning. There are lots of "interesting" things you can study and a lot more things that ultimately are little more than "trivia." A good group leader can discern between what is "interesting" from what is "important" and what is meaningful. Therefore, narrow your dialogical learning objectives to those things that will actually make a difference in the lives of your learners. The kinds of learning objectives that make a difference tend to be those that address an *immediate need* your learners have expressed or you have identified by observation or through your relationship with them. To consistently deal only in the "interesting" and "trivial," no matter how entertaining, ultimately trivializes your students' concept of the faith. Faith matters, and meaningful learning objectives help the group members realize that what they learn makes a difference in their lives.

We will conclude this chapter by examining additional sample dialogical learning outcomes that can be used in the small group study context. To develop your skill, check each outcome against the checklist. Once you have spent some time studying these samples, write at least three dialogical learning outcomes for your next small group study.

At the conclusion of this session, group members will be able to

1. demonstrate an understanding of the basic concept of reconciliation by identifying three basic elements of the concept;

2. articulate the difference between reconciliation and the related concepts of forgiveness and revenge; and

3. identify the value of using reconciliation in specific personal relationships as a foundational concept over other related concepts.

In this session, the group members will be able to

1. describe three examples of pastoral crisis intervention they have experienced and cite at least one of three biblical examples of pastoral care intervention;

2. identify two principles of pastoral crisis intervention found in a case study; and

3. demonstrate one pastoral care skill characterized by sound biblical principles learned today.

At the conclusion of this class, group members will be able to

1. identify four of the six factors that are obstacles to hospitality communication;

2. apply biblical principles of hospitality communication in a role play situation; and

3. assess the effective use of hospitality communication in a group study session.

At the completion of this group study, members will

1. correctly identify five out of seven components of leadership through self-differentiation;

2. correctly list five potential reactivity postures to self-differentiating leadership stances; and

3. predict how a self-differentiated leader would respond to statements of dissent in a case study.

CHAPTER 6

Effective Small Group
Learning Methods

This chapter provides a catalog of techniques that are suitable for small group study using the dialogical learning approach. In this chapter you will find a repertoire of methods that are leader-directed but learner-focused and can be used for most subject matter, including the Bible, since they allow for good group process and dialogical learning. Some of these techniques will help make the group orientation or instructional time efficient, memorable, and fun. Some can be used within the larger dialogical learning group format (15 to 20 group members) to keep things moving, to facilitate small group management, or to make dialogical learning interaction fun.

When group members understand the use and purpose of a new method, they are likely to be willing to try it and use it correctly. Nothing brings the group learning process to a screeching halt faster than confusion among the group members about what it is they are supposed to do. So whenever you introduce a new method to the group, be sure to provide directions, model the method, and explain what it is intended to do for the group. And remember, a method is only effective if there is a specific purpose for using *that* method and not another to achieve a learning outcome. Using a method just because you think it is "interesting" or "fun" for the group, without any connection to helping your group achieve its goal for learning, can actually impede the learning process.

Before moving on to specific techniques for facilitating a dialogical learning group, review the general guidelines. Remember that dialogical learning is a specific educational process, and therefore, we should think about it as "rigid." By rigid, I mean we should respect the necessity of sticking with the process, because process facilitates learning. More often than not, when we take shortcuts in the learning process, we sabotage its effectiveness.

General Guidelines for Leading a Dialogical Learning Group

1. State the group learning objective or goal clearly (unless discovery or creative dissonance is part of the learning experience, in which case, keep them guessing until the debriefing time). Try to limit the group dialogical learning assignment to a single goal, or two related goals at most. Be specific about what you are asking group members to do.

2. Outline the process for the small group assignment. Sometimes you will want to provide specific steps or a particular procedure for the group to follow. For reference, outline the steps on a chalkboard, poster, PowerPoint, or handout for the groups.

3. Provide the groups with any resources they will need as part of their dialogical learning assignments or activities, including writing instruments, note paper, research materials, or handouts.

4. Give a time limit. Provide groups a sufficient amount of time to complete assignments or to engage in discussion. For most small group dialogical learning experiences, you'll find that a minimum of 40 minutes is required for a group of four or five, longer if the group is larger. If you find that most breakout groups, within a larger group or class setting, have finished the assignment, go ahead and call time to maintain the lesson momentum and avoid distractions and downtime.

5. Monitor the groups during their dialogical learning process time. When working with small groups within a larger group setting, walk around and eavesdrop on the group dialogue. This will help the groups stay on task and will make you available to clarify procedure or content questions. This will also make you available to help "sick" groups— those that cannot seem to get on with the task at hand, are stuck with a monopolizing group member, get sidetracked from the discussion, or find themselves made up of people who don't readily join in.

6. Debrief and evaluate. Always debrief your small groups to affirm the value of the work they have done and to carry small group learning experiences into the larger class grouping. Ask clarifying and summarizing questions, and use a flip chart or chalkboard to record responses from the smaller groups.[1]

Now let's examine specific methods that you can use in the group dialogical learning context. They include methods for managing groups, getting a group's attention and keeping the group focused, promoting group interaction, getting your group members talking, using body language, fostering critical thinking, telling a Bible story or interpreting a passage, and using music. You probably already use some of these methods in your teaching. Challenge yourself to add to your repertoire by applying some of these methods as appropriate. Remember that a method is only as good as its ability to help your group achieve its learning objective.

• **Methods for Group Management.** Methods for group management are not "educational" methods as such, but they are very important for undergirding and facilitating a good dialogical learning experience. Group management methods are those that are concerned with "housekeeping," removing obstacles to learning, or making the learning experience a smooth process free from distractions. These group management methods are primarily teacher and leader tasks, although many can be assigned or delegated to group members.

1. Set the environment. One way the group facilitator can demonstrate and practice servant leadership is by taking upon himself or herself the grunt work of ensuring that the group learning environment is ready to receive the group members. Leaders should arrive early to do such things as prepare the seating arrangement, remove distractions, set the thermostat, tidy up the room, and get the coffee ready. A comfortable environment can go a long way toward making dialogical learning pleasant and effective, and an uncomfortable learning environment can distract members and sabotage the best-designed learning experience.

2. Keep supplies handy. Because dialogical learning often is complex and multidimensional, your group may need to have access to learning resources for consultation and study. Keep supplies such as Bibles, pencils and paper, and reference works accessible to the group.

3. Assign housekeeping tasks. Getting group members to help with group management tasks can be very helpful. Many hands make light work, as they say. Assign or call for volunteers to be responsible for arranging chairs before and after meetings, making coffee, distributing supplies, taking attendance, and sending e-mail notices to group members.

4. Establish procedures. Establishing procedures for mundane housekeeping tasks will go a long way toward removing distractions and will make for smoother beginnings and endings to the dialogical learning experience. For example, you can establish procedures for making announcements, making copies, locking doors, putting away chairs, and distributing materials.

5. Anticipate interruptions. Take time to anticipate the many kinds of interruptions your group may face (alarm bells, noise from an adjacent classroom or meeting room, coffee-corner cleanup, running out of handouts, media equipment failure, a latecomer, not enough chairs for latecomers, or a cell phone going off). Then, decide on actions you can take to smoothly address these interruptions before they derail the group dialogical learning experience. You can assign responsibility to specific group members to deal with these interruptions, or emergencies, to help you stay focused on facilitating the group while the interruption is addressed.

6. Maintain expectations of group norms. One of the most important, but often neglected, group management functions of the group leader is to maintain the expectations of group norms as needed. For example, if class members start arriving tardy to the group meetings, and if the group covenant includes "being on time" (and even if it doesn't), then the group facilitator needs to do some "housekeeping" by reminding the group members of the importance of commitment to the group and the necessity of being on time. The watchful group leader will spot when things start unraveling and will address these group management issues early, before they become a major disruption to the group's ability to learn together.

• **Methods for Attention and Focus.** Once, when I worked as a school principal, I was debriefing a student teacher about her experiences at our school. She had been shadowing one of our teachers and her class for three weeks. At one point, I asked her what surprises, if any, she encountered in her observations.

She replied, "I was really amazed at how much time the class spends outside of the classroom, what with bathroom breaks, lunch and snack breaks, playground break, computer lab, physical education, and traveling through the halls to all those places. It's a wonder they get any learning during the day!"

In education, the term "instructional time" refers to the time during which teaching and learning takes place exclusive of other activities, such as moving from place to place, classroom management, discipline, bathroom breaks, and distributing supplies. Observing the actual amount of "instructional time" children get during the course of a normal school day can be alarming. On a good day, most schoolchildren get at most about three hours of actual "instruction time." This is why effective class management is critical. When you have only so much time to give instruction in a day, you had better make it good!

Now think about the amount of "instructional time"—the time spent on actual teaching and learning activities—you have on a typical Sunday morning or Wednesday evening. Though many Sunday schools, for instance, run from 9:45 to 10:45, actual teaching-learning time is probably less than 40 minutes on a good Sunday. That's 40 minutes of formal religious instruction out of an entire week for most learners! In that context, mastering techniques for effective group management becomes critical to allow the time needed for dialogical learning.

The key to effective group control is to be able to get your learners' attention with a minimum of effort. Teacher behaviors—like getting your group underway, changing the direction of group activities, or reconvening your group after an interruption in learning activities— are critical to your success in managing the group process. A common mistake among inexperienced teachers is starting to teach before getting everyone's attention, or moving prematurely into activities before learners are in a proper mental state. Initiative, or attention-getting, techniques are preconditions to effective learning and good group process. Mastering these techniques can help get your study group under control from the start and enhance the learning experience of the group members. There are four basic types of initiative group management techniques: *cuing, tuning, pausing,* and *restarting.*

1. Cuing. Effective nonverbal cues are great in helping learners know what is going on with a minimal amount of distraction. Cuing may involve standing in front of the class, manipulating an object, or raising your hand as a signal for quiet. Of course, you will have to let your learners know early on what these nonverbal cues mean (e.g., "When I raise my hand like this, I need all eyes on me with your full attention and no talking"). The essence of good group management in dialogical learning is getting your learners to work cooperatively and productively in a group setting; therefore, a large part of cuing amounts to conditioning learners to respond appropriately with certain behaviors to your signals. You can imagine the amount of time and stress you can save by training group members to simultaneously perform necessary behaviors with a minimum of commotion, distraction, or resistance.

2. Tuning. Sometimes nonverbal cues are ineffective, so it is necessary to use verbal cues to get the group's attention. This can be simply facing the class and making a statement in emphatic terms (remember, you're in charge of the overall group process), such as, "I'd like everyone's attention, please." Once you have everyone's attention, you can proceed—but do not proceed before everyone is focused on you. When your learners appear ready to begin without more prompting, move directly into the orientation step in the lesson with a concise statement: "I have a question I've been thinking about . . ." or "I wonder how many of you have heard of this before . . ." or "I want you to raise your hand when responding to this question." Whatever means you use to tune your study group in on you, make a special effort to get the whole group in sync with you at the beginning of the class period as well as during transition times.

3. Pausing. Pauses can generally be used to good advantage when you want to get your group's attention. Use pauses to momentarily wait out group members when they are vying for attention, are all wanting to give an answer at the same time, or are slow to regather into a large group for debriefing. This is a low-key technique designed to provide a slight jar to inattentive learners. However, this technique works only when you have been engaged in a normal course of conversational teaching. For the pause to work best, it is followed by nonverbal cues that communicate, "I'm waiting," "Please give your attention up here," or "As soon as everyone is ready I'll continue." You'll usually need to wait several seconds for learners to focus their attention on you during a pause. However, allowing learners to ignore the meaning of your pause will only encourage distracting behavior, so be sure to enforce the response you expect when you use this technique.

4. Restarting. Restarting is another form of pausing, though potentially less effective if not used correctly. In restarting you stop talking in the middle of a sentence and restart as a sign of refusal to accept inattention. For example, "I'd like to read a verse . . . I'd like to read . . . I'd like to . . ." This subtle technique will usually get the group's attention when used right. If several attempts at restarting fail to get your group's attention, it's usually a good sign that a short break is needed or a stronger refocusing technique is called for.

To move your group members' dialogue along, either at transition points in your lesson or when starting the session, you first need to get everyone's attention. Now that we have identified the four types of initiative techniques that you can use to get your group's attention or to help them focus, here are ten specific techniques you can use to get your group's attention. Watch for the "law of diminishing effect," however. If you notice the class starting to ignore the signal you have been using, it may be time to change to a different instrument or sound or to switch to another attention-getting technique.

1. Shout. But don't shout in desperation. A "group shout" will get everyone focused and participating. If one or two learners do not participate, tell the class (not the individuals) that they didn't shout loud enough and have them try again. Obviously, you don't want to try this too often.

2. Play music. Play a rousing piece of marching music or a catchy guitar riff. Train your class that this is a signal to "stop and listen." You can also train your group members to listen for quiet music as a signal to settle into a reading or prayer time or to regather into a large group for debriefing or orientation.

3. Clap in rhythm. To get your class's attention, begin clapping in rhythm and signal for them to follow along. You can give instructions for the next step in your lesson by speaking in keeping with the rhythm: "Put (*clap*) your (*clap*) papers (*clap*) down (*clap*) and (*clap*) move (*clap*) your (*clap*) chairs (*clap*) in (*clap*) a (*clap*) circle."

4. Sing instructions. Singing is very effective with children but can also get the attention of a group of adults having trouble moving on to the next step in your lesson. You don't need a good singing voice to use this method; remember that your goal is to get their attention.

5. Raise your hand. This is very effective especially if you train your group to raise their hands also in response and then pay attention. By using this method, you will not have to raise your voice, and the group will help by getting the attention of anyone who hasn't raised his or her hand.

6. Show an object. Use an object as a point of focus and to signal that the class should pay attention to you. Your object can be a surprise you pull out from under a table, a large sealed brown paper bag you place on the table to create intrigue, or something your class is trained to respond to, like a "talking stick" (see page 74). You can also use a splash screen on a PowerPoint slide or unveil a poster.

7. Whisper. As a rule, whispering is a more powerful attention-getter than raising your voice. Talk in a low voice as you give instructions or directions and watch how your group members strain to pay attention. Once they are focused on you, talk in a normal voice.

8. Play an instrument. Even if you are not proficient at it, tooting on a wind instrument, playing a chord on a keyboard, or even chiming a bell will get the attention of your group members. If you can break into a transitioning song, all the better.

9. Tap on shoulder. Quietly tapping your learners on the shoulder and maintaining eye contact can get the attention of one or two learners, such as the small group discussion leaders, without disrupting the rest of the class. Or you can go around and tap all of the group members on the shoulder and have them follow you to the next learning station if the study involves moving to different areas.

10. Turn off the lights. This old technique is a bit abrupt, but it still works. Turn the lights off then on in the classroom to get attention, and give your directions immediately. As with all stimulus-response techniques, this one can lose its effectiveness if used too often.

Remember that the goal of these techniques is to help facilitate dialogical learning. So be sure to be intentional about why you use these techniques and at what point in the learning process they will be most helpful for getting your group members into the dialogue.

• **Methods for Interaction.** The following techniques can be used to help your learners become more active participants in the group learning experience. These techniques for interaction facilitate sharing of ideas, gaining insight, and inviting people into dialogue. Use at least one participation method per class session and you will see a difference in your learners' level of group interaction and an increase in their rate of retention of what they are studying.

1. Discussion starter. A discussion starter can take the form of almost anything you can relate to the lesson at hand: newspaper articles, an object or artifact, case studies, a simple story, an anecdote or parable, a video clip, a graphic, or a leading open-ended question.[2]

2. Poetry reading. Reading and responding to a poem is helpful in moving learners to imagery, interpretation, and emotional responses to ideas, and to using analogies and metaphors. Poetry is also a great way to tap into the affective domain of feelings and emotions.

3. Time lines. Having group members make a time line as they explore historical events, interpret a case study, or tell their own life stories will help them put things in context and understand relationships among events, ideas, and persons.

4. Pro-con analysis. Present learners with a problem. Suggest a solution to the problem and have them analyze the pros and cons of the proposed solution. See if they can come up with a better solution.

5. Group games. Games can be used at any stage of the lesson: charades, Password, situations, Pictionary, card exchange, Concentration, Jeopardy, Bible quiz bowl. However, remember that even games need to be purposeful and help you achieve the learning outcome.

6. Acrostic. At the beginning or end of the lesson, have the group members make an acrostic of a key word or phrase of the lesson. To create an acrostic, write the letters that spell out a word vertically from top to bottom. Then, in crossword puzzle fashion, create associated words that begin with the first letter of each of the letters that make up the key word. Have them explain how their chosen words relate to the central idea. For example, an acrostic of the word "dialogue" might look like this:

Discourse
I ntrospective
Active learning
Lively
On-going
Great for Bible study
Understanding deeper
Exciting

7. Paraphrase. To help the group members get to the meaning of a passage, have them interpret the passage by paraphrasing it (putting it in their own words). Assign the work to small groups—dyads or triads—and compare paraphrases for discussion.

8. *True-false statements.* Have group members respond to a series of true and false statements. Deliberately ambiguous statements are great for discussion starters and for facilitating interaction.

• **Methods for Getting Your Group Members Talking.** One of the deadliest things you can do to make the learning process come to a screeching halt is to invite the class members into a vacuum, gathering the group around nothing—no focus, no procedure, no intent. For groups to move ahead, they need direction, structure, and a kick-start to get them going. Here are some techniques to use to help your group members start talking and ease into the dialogical learning experience.

1. *Use a "talking stick."* A talking stick is an ancient dialogue technique used in many cultures. After a topic of discussion or a problem is presented to the group, the talking stick is passed around the circle from one person to the next (either in turn around a circle or selectively). Whoever has the stick must speak to the issue at hand; everyone else listens. Or when someone wants to share a thought, he or she must ask for the talking stick. Once everyone has shared, someone can ask for the talking stick to speak or respond. A talking stick can be anything from a large wooden spoon to a craft stick. For added fun, use a big stick with elaborate decoration.

2. *Use agree-disagree cards.* This is a good large group activity to use before breaking up into smaller dialogical learning groups. Write various opinions about a given topic on 3 x 5 cards. You'll need at least three cards for each person. Shuffle the cards and distribute them to the group. Instruct the group members to read each card, to decide whether they agree or disagree with the statement, and to tell why. Next, have the members try to give away any cards with which they disagree and trade for cards with which they agree. They do this by telling the other person why they feel and think as they do.

3. *Use case studies.* Case studies are great ways to get people talking. Write a brief case study related to the topic under discussion. You can make it open-ended and controversial but realistic. Give enough concrete information for your group to work with. Give the group two or three (at most, four) questions to deal with based on the situation. You

can break the class into groups with each taking on a different point of view or answering a different set of questions. Debrief with the large group afterward. (See appendix F for guidelines on writing a case study.)

4. *Play "What If?"* To help your learners look at things differently and expand the conversation among the participants, play "What If?" To play, read a passage of Scripture or focus on the topic at hand and prompt your learners to come up with as many "What if?" questions as they can. Anything goes, but once you have compiled a list, choose one or two "What if?" scenarios to explore.

5. *Play "But I'd Like Your Opinion."* This technique uses an object similar to the talking stick, but instead of group members asking for the object, they give it to another to hear his or her opinion. You can start by giving your opinion about the Bible passage, issue, or topic under discussion. When you have shared your thoughts, say, "But I'd like your opinion," and pass the object (a talking stick, a ball, a wooden block) to another class member. That person shares, then passes the object on to another, saying, "But I'd like to hear your opinion." Depending on the subject, question, or learning objective, you can give participants the option to "pass" (or to pass only once). At the end of this activity, debrief the class on the opinions shared and continue with the discussion or with the next step in the lesson.

• **Methods Using Didactic Body Language.** The Gospel of Matthew records that Jesus said, "Every day I sat in the temple courts teaching" (26:55, NIV). And Mark tells us, "Again Jesus began to teach by the lake. The crowd that gathered around him was so large that he got into a boat and sat in it out on the lake, while all the people were along the shore at the water's edge. He taught them many things by parables" (4:1-2, NIV). You're probably familiar with those verses, but have you ever associated the body language with the corresponding action? In both verses, Jesus *sits* to *teach*. In Jesus' culture, teachers sat while teaching. It is no accident that both Gospel writers noted Jesus' posture as being significant—when Jesus sat before a group of people, he was teaching, and what he was about to say was important.

Teaching is a multimedia event, even without hi-tech equipment. We teach by what we say, show, and do—and by what we *don't* say, show, and do! Effective teachers understand the importance of didactic body language and learn to use it as efficiently as any other teaching method. When I was a school principal, I would often hear veteran teachers half-jokingly tell the new teachers, "Don't smile until December." And perhaps you remember knowing you were in trouble when your teacher or parent gave you "that look." I've seen teachers silence an entire class of second graders with "that look." Quite impressive!

Here's what we know: if a small group leader demonstrates positive nonverbal communication, learners react favorably and learn better. The same is true in dialogical learning when group members learn from each other. Dialogical learning involves not only what group members say, but *how* they say it through nonverbal cues. Unless we were reared in closets or were wolf-children, most of us know the basic vocabulary of body language.

- A smile gives positive feedback and impacts the affective domain by communicating pleasure, trust, friendliness, interest, excitement, or surprise.

- A deadpan expression communicates distrust, low energy, or disinterest.

- A frown communicates displeasure, disapproval, and anger; but combine a frown with holding your chin or scratching your head, and it can be a sign that you are thinking or puzzled.

- Standing with your arms crossed is a defensive gesture.

- Sitting with your legs crossed communicates nervousness and guardedness, while sitting with your arms and legs crossed means there's no convincing you!

- Avoiding eye contact means disinterest, lack of confidence, uncertainty, or lying.

- Staring signals suspicion or anger. (When someone is sitting cross-legged, cross-armed, frowning, and staring, it's a good time to give up trying to teach. That person is not willing to learn!)

The following chart presents some proven didactic body language techniques for leading small groups. The secret to using them effectively is to (1) be aware of how you use your body language in communicating and conscious of how it comes across to your learners, and (2) expand your didactic language vocabulary by practicing some of these techniques and keeping the ones that work best for you.

Body Language Techniques

To get your learners' attention, try the following:

- Walk to the front of the room.

- Stand at attention.

- Survey the group and make eye contact.

- Hold up your hand.

- Tap a desk, turn the lights off then on, or ring a bell.

- Use appropriate facial expression (frown, smile).

- Shrug your shoulders.

- Make an appropriate hand gesture (like the universal "okay" or "thumbs-up" signs).

To invite a particular learner to participate in an activity, try one of these:

- Smile at the designated learner.

- Focus your eyes on the learner.

- Nod at the learner.

- Turn your body toward the learner.

- Point to the learner.

- Walk toward the learner.

- Touch the learner on the shoulder.

(Note: While the following category may seem inappropriate for leading adults, I've actually found these techniques more helpful with adults than with children since some adults seem unable to grow out of their scripts from when they were children in a classroom.)

To deal with interruptive learner behavior in the group, try these:

- Turn your body toward and focus your eyes on the off-task learner.

- Frown at the learner.

- Raise your eyebrows.

- Wave your hand at the offending learner.

- Point your finger at the learner.

- Walk toward the misbehaving learner.

- Put your hand firmly on the shoulder of the acting-out learner.

- Put your hand on the desk or back of the chair of the inattentive learner.

- Sit down near the learner.

- Touch the object the learner is touching.

• **Methods for Fostering Critical Thinking.** Socrates said, "The unexamined life is not worth living." Likewise, an unexamined faith is not worth much either. One of the most important characteristics of mature faith is the ability to critically examine one's beliefs, values, assumptions, and prejudices. Author and screenwriter Wilson Mizner said, "I respect faith; but doubt is what gets you an education." You will want to include a time of debriefing and closure when using any of the following methods. Here are some activities to help your group members think critically as they engage in dialogical learning:

1. *Choose items from a list.* Choosing from a list, through prioritizing or elimination, forces learners to create criteria for choosing. Follow up by asking the learners to explain the rationale for their choices and how they arrived at that rationale. You can have individual group members choose from the list and compare and contrast with the other group members, or you can invite the group to work toward a concensus. Either method will facilitate interesting dialogue and discussion.

2. *Work a puzzle.* Working on a puzzle requires several thinking modalities. Puzzles are a good warm-up activity for critical thinking sessions. Puzzles can be solved individually or as a group effort. Invite the learners to explain how they went about solving the puzzle—intuition, logic, experience, inductive or deductive reasoning? The variety and types of puzzles are endless. You can use a puzzle for almost every lesson and never run out! You can use crossword puzzles, word-search puzzles, block puzzles, story puzzles, riddle puzzles, knot puzzles, physical activity puzzles, game puzzles, logic puzzles, paper and pencil puzzles, or math puzzles.

3. *Match items in one list with items in another.* Matching items forces learners to look for shared qualities, a basic component to understanding concepts. The phrase "class of objects" refers to the parts or components that make up a given concept. We understand a concept when we can identify the class of objects that belong to the concept or that constitute the concept, that is, when we can say "Yes, that belongs to this concept" or "No, this does not belong to this concept." For example, some concepts, such as "home," are inclusive in that all kinds of things can belong to them. Other concepts, on the other hand, are more closely defined by components—of what must be included and what cannot be included for something or someone to belong to that concept. One example of a complex concept is "Christian." There are

many identifiers that make someone or something (a church or an enterprise, for example) Christian. Additionally, there are restrictive components—aspects that, if present, exclude the person or thing from being Christian. If this idea sounds complex, it is, but it's important to understand because, let's face it, faith necessitates understanding some pretty heavy concepts, such as love, hope, faith, redemption, good, evil, eternity, and salvation.

4. Carry out an experiment. The process of carrying out an experiment calls upon the learners to use the entire gamut of cognitive skills: knowledge, comprehension, application, analysis, synthesis, and evaluation. Conducting an experiment facilitates critical thinking when you end the activity by asking group members to form a conclusion, make an inference, or predict the results of modified experiments with different factors and variables.

5. Engage in thematic apperception dialogue. In this method, group members examine a picture of people interacting in some context and describe and interpret what is going on and what the people are thinking and feeling. Additionally, you can ask the group to make up a story surrounding the situation they see depicted. Follow-up dialogue allows group members to work on critical self-awareness of perception, assumptions, and prejudices.

6. Judge the merit of an argument. Judging forces learners to form an idea or opinion on the matter at hand. It calls on learners to draw on previous knowledge and personal experience and to take seriously another person's point of view. This activity also helps bring to the surface criteria, values, or assumptions people hold—often uncritically or unaware—that they draw on when ascribing value or forming an opinion.

7. Critique a poem, story, painting, film clip (perhaps a television commercial or a segment from a movie), book (or book review), essay, popular song lyric, or article. Critiquing forces the learner to actively engage with ideas and assumptions behind works rather than uncritically accepting the messages and values behind those works.

8. Compare similar ideas, items, or arguments. Comparing similar ideas forces the learner to pick up the nuances of arguments and get behind the motivations for those arguments. This is especially useful in helping learners work at moral reasoning and theological or ethical positions people take.

9. Predict the outcome of a situation. Predicting an outcome causes learners to weigh determining factors, draw on experience, spot trends and patterns, and deal with factors imagined but yet unknown. This can lead to lively dialogue as group members challenge each other to give a rationale for their thinking. Predicting an outcome can be an effective way to conclude a case study.

10. Revise a story or article. Revising stories or articles fosters the ability to think of alternatives to presented ideas. It allows learners to develop counterarguments as they critically assess a point of view or conclusion.

• **Methods for Telling a Bible Story or Interpreting a Passage.** Very often the focus of your study will be a Bible passage. There are more ways to introduce the Bible text than just reading it, although you should read the passage at some point regardless of how creatively you choose to present it. Below are just a few ways you can introduce a Bible passage to the group. Some of these techniques can also be used as methods to interpret the biblical text.

1. Read it dramatically. For a Bible passage that is in story form, you can assign parts to group members and read the text as a drama.

2. Act it out. For a dramatic text or Bible story, learners can work from the text or a prepared script (a script they create) or simply improvise. They can act out the story using spoken dialogue or pantomime.

3. Show it. There are many good videos of biblical scenes, stories, and passages. One good technique for exploring the details of a text is to have group members compare a video version with the text as it is written.

4. Play a performance. A performance is an interpretation of the text and thus is ideal for dialogical learning. A performance can be in one of many forms, for example, a puppet show (live or taped) or music, such as *Messiah* by Handel, *Elijah* by Mendelssohn, or *St. Matthew's Passion* by Bach.

5. Compare it. The interpretation of a Bible passage often resides in its literary form (e.g., poetry, story, or letter). Comparing passages of Scripture for literary forms is a good dialogical exercise for interpretation. Sometimes you can compare a passage of Scripture with a secular piece of literature of the same form.

6. Picture it. You can also "show" the Bible text through art or graphics. There are endless sources of graphics material, including the library, the Internet, or a resource center, in an endless variety of media, from flannel board (yes, old fashioned educational technologies can be as effective as new hi-tech ones!) to paintings.

7. Draw it. Asking group members to draw a Bible passage is a powerful form of interpretation. They can draw in any media and use any number of styles, such as portrait, abstract, or cartoon strip.

8. Paraphrase it. Another effective form of interpretation is having group members put the Bible passage into their own words. You can also use a paraphrased Bible version to contrast a more text-based translation.

9. Sing it. Many Bible passages, from Psalms to laments to proverbs, can be sung. Even the names of the disciples have been set to music. Consult your church's hymnal for hymns and songs based on Bible texts. Don't forget that another form of "singing" is antiphonal reading, such as responsive readings.

10. Take it apart. Ask the group to analyze a Bible story or passage by "taking it apart" to examine the smaller components that make up the passage.

11. Put it together. After you take apart a biblical text through analysis, it often is helpful to put it back together for a reinterpretation. Other ways to have your group members put it together is to print out a passage of Scripture text, distribute sections, and see if they can put it together correctly. Or, you can distribute portions (verses) of two different texts and see if they can correctly put the corresponding passages together. This can be a good exercise for comparing and contrasting Synoptic Gospel passages of the same event.

• **Methods for Using Music in the Small Study Group.** Music is a part of the daily lives of most of our learners. It seems strange, therefore, that we do not incorporate it into our teaching more often. Music has been shown to be an aid to learning.[3] Furthermore, music speaks to the domain where the Spirit is most at home within us: our affective domain. Here are ten ways to use music in your small group to facilitate dialogical learning.

1. Play a recording. Enhance your group's learning experience by playing music as background for small group work. Highlight a particular song that relates to the lesson. Play contemporary popular songs and have your group members think critically about the content of the lyrics.

2. Have a performance. You probably have some hidden musical talent in your small groups. Encourage your group members to use their musical skill in the lesson. Explore ways talents and gifts relate, the value of the discipline of practice, and ways music speaks to a person's spiritual life.

3. Write a hymn. Use the tune of a familiar hymn and have your group members write new lyrics relating to the topic they are studying.

4. Sing a song. Start your learning session with a rousing song to stir things up, or end your session with a quiet, meditative song or familiar hymn.

5. Tap out a rhythm. Help your group members memorize a passage of Scripture, a key quote, a proverb, or a saying by having them tap out the rhythm of the words. Repeat until they have learned the passage by heart.

6. Play musical chairs. Musical chairs is a good experiential activity when you are studying topics or Bible passages related to being left out, being late, failing to listen, feeling anxious, or being competitive. Playing a game breaks up a long study session, gets the group pumped up, and injects a little fun into the learning experience.

7. Play a note code puzzle. Teach your group members the letter names of notes (ABCDEFG) and have them create or solve a letter substitution puzzle.

8. Create a band. Provide rhythm instruments, harmonicas, kazoos, tambourines, and the like, and lead the group members in a performance to express celebration or as a way to teach cooperation. Form two groups and challenge them to make up lyrics as you go along.

9. Circle dance. Circle dances are simple to learn and provide a wonderful mix of music, text, and movement. Provide lots of space, or if weather permits, perform outside.

10. Contrast music styles. Introduce your learners to different ethnic music, religious and secular "spiritual" music, classical music, and contemporary music. Invite your learners to contrast the styles, explore ways the styles communicate and elicit emotions, and discuss how some styles feel more familiar than others.

PART 2
Dialogical Studies Illustrated

CHAPTER 7

A Dialogical Learning Book Study Illustrated

The dialogical learning approach to small group study can be used for Bible study or for a book study. In congregations, these are the two areas of study that most small groups use. This chapter and the next will provide sample group sessions using the dialogical learning approach. This chapter contains a sample of a dialogical learning approach to a book study. Chapter 8 presents a sample dialogical learning Bible study, and chapter 9 has a sample dialogical learning topical study. These three chapters are examples of how the dialogical small group learning method can be structured in the form of a lesson or a class session. By studying these three types of studies (a book study, a Bible study, and a topical study) in the form of a "teaching plan," you will be able to see how the dialogical learning approach can be structured for use in the small group setting. As you examine these examples, make note of the structure of the lesson, the methods used, the types of dialogical questions asked, and the flow of the lesson.

The sample dialogical learning lesson in this chapter is for a study of the book *10 Best Parenting Ways to Ruin Your Teenager* by Israel Galindo and Don Reagan (Richmond, VA: Educational Consultants, 2005; it may be purchased from www.galindoconsultants.com, where you can download the entire eight-session dialogical learning group study guide). In this book study, parents make up the small group, typically between six and eight members. When the group is larger, for example, from 18 to 20 members, the participants form smaller dialogical learning groups of four or five for the discussions. The participants read the book chapter ahead of time so that they come prepared with questions, ideas, and opinions.

The dialogical learning approach presented in this chapter strives to (1) help participants interact with each other through dialogue, and (2) connect content to life through the sharing of personal life stories and experiences. At times the experiences solicited are from the person's past, and at other times the experiences called for are about a current life situation. Further, the dialogical learning experience is informed by two intentional goals:

1. to help the parent participants incorporate an insight (which is overtly presented at the beginning of the session) through group dialogue, and

2. to apply the insight to their experience, which is realized by the "Going Deeper" part of the lesson.

The learning session samples are for group sessions 2 and 3. It is assumed that in the first session, the groups have been formed and a group covenant (see appendix B) has been agreed to. Additionally, it is expected that the group facilitator has spent some time training the members in good group learning skills. Good group learning experiences do not happen naturally; they are a result of intentional and responsible behaviors by group members. So a good group must be taught and trained to be a good group, and that is the job of the group leader or facilitator. You can create and use a handout similar to the one on the next page (see also appendix K) to orient group members and establish norms and values during the initial orientation meetings. Posting the information can serve as a reminder to members as the study progresses.

With the group covenant in place and having reviewed good group skills, the group will be able to jump right into the dialogical learning experience with little prompting. You will notice in the session outlines that there is no teaching-by-telling time and very little direction from the group facilitator. In fact, all the directions the group needs are provided on the group discussion handouts. By this stage, the group facil-

How to Be a Good Group Member

A good group depends on the good will and participation of its members. Remember, a group is only as good as its weakest member—don't be that person in your group!

A good group member . . .
- comes to meetings on time
- supports the work of the group
- shares ideas
- takes responsibilities for duties assigned
- believes in the significance of the work
- communicates honestly
- demonstrates accountability
- recognizes his or her strengths and limitations
- determines to be honest and transparent with others in the group
- participates in dialogue and discussion
- takes time to think
- listens to what other members say
- gives reasons for his or her answers
- stays on the task or on the topic under discussion
- allows himself or herself to be challenged in order to grow
- can negotiate the level of confidentiality he or she needs
- asks thought-provoking questions
- asks for others' opinions
- asks, "How does this apply to me?"
- asks, "What am I learning?"

itator's function is to set up the environment, provide resources, help the groups start and end on time, be a resource for the group when process questions arise, and most important, simply allow the dialogical learning process to happen!

These sessions can run from an hour to 90 minutes. Notice that for that time frame, which can be considered "generous" by comparison to the times allotted for most learning events in church, there are *only three dialogical questions* per session. This allows the time needed for dialogical learning to happen. Groups using this guide have reported that sometimes they have difficulty getting to the learning activities because they are so involved in sharing through dialogue! If the group is a larger group of 15 to 20 persons who break up into smaller study units for the dialogical learning session, the group facilitator can call for a debriefing time at the end of the session. This allows the smaller groups to share insights, questions, and challenges for the benefit of the whole. Remember, however, that debriefing questions are intentionally about summarizing, soliciting insights, and bringing home the learning intent of the session.

Sample Session Outlines

SESSION 2
The Second Best Way to Ruin Your Teenager Is to Parent Your Teenager as If He or She Is an Adult

Directions

Read chapter 2 of *10 Best Parenting Ways To Ruin Your Teenager* by Galindo and Reagan in preparation for this session.

Before you begin, choose a timekeeper-prompter for your group. This person will help your group stay on task and will keep things moving along by monitoring the time and by asking follow-up questions. You do not have to answer all of the discussion questions listed; choose those that are of most interest to your group members. For optimum discussion time, form a group of four or five persons.

Parenting Insights for This Session

- Treating your teenager like an adult will confuse your teenager by removing too quickly the boundaries he or she needs in place to learn about the world.

- Your teenager is on his or her way to becoming an adult—but is not there yet.

- Teenagers think and "feel" things differently.

Discussion Questions

1. Do you remember when you first realized that you were "grown up"? Share a story of that moment. Where were you when you had that insight? Was there an incident that caused you to "grow up" and become an adult? Do you think you "grew up" too fast? Not fast enough?

2. Do you think teenagers "grow up" too fast today? Give examples of where and how you see that to be true. If you don't think that that is true, explain why.

3. Share from your experience the way(s) you perceive that teenagers don't "think like adults." Describe a conversation or an incident with your teenager in which this became evident.

Learning Activity

Divide the class into two groups, Group A and Group B. Provide a flip chart, poster board, or a large piece of paper and markers for each group. Distribute handouts and have the groups record their responses on the flip chart. Debrief by having each group report their responses. Share the implications for parenting teenagers from the insights they gain from this exercise.

Note: The following handouts would be reproduced and distributed to the appropriate groups.

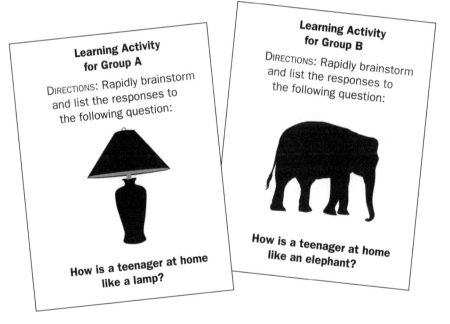

Learning Activity for Group A

DIRECTIONS: Rapidly brainstorm and list the responses to the following question:

How is a teenager at home like a lamp?

Learning Activity for Group B

DIRECTIONS: Rapidly brainstorm and list the responses to the following question:

How is a teenager at home like an elephant?

Going Deeper

Sit down with your teenagers and share with them, in detail, how you were as a teenager. Describe the friends you had and the feelings you experienced, and describe the way you dressed and looked. Share your recollection about your religious or spiritual beliefs at the time. When you are done, invite your teenager to ask you any question about you as a teenager—and answer honestly.

SESSION 3
The Third Best Way to Ruin Your Teenager
Is to Be Inflexible with Rules

Directions

Read chapter 3 of *10 Best Parenting Ways to Ruin Your Teenager* by Galindo and Reagan in preparation for this session.

Before you begin, choose a timekeeper-prompter for your group. This person will help your group stay on task and will keep things moving along by monitoring the time and by asking follow-up questions. You do not have to answer all of the discussion questions listed; choose those that are of most interest to your group members. For optimum discussion time, form a group of four or five persons.

Parenting Insights for This Session

- Teenagers need new and different rules than when they were children.

- Increase your teenager's freedom, when it is earned, but with increased responsibility.

- Setting limits and boundaries remains an important part of the parent-teen relationship.

Discussion Questions

1. What rules did you have in your family of origin when you were a child? What rules did you have to abide by when you were a teenager? As you look back, did any of the rules not make sense?

2. Are there rules in place in your relationship with your children and teenagers that you borrowed from your own family of origin? What are they? Why are these rules important to you? Finally, do these rules "work" for your family?

3. Share occasions when you have had conflict with your teenager regarding rules. What was the rule, what was the occasion, and how were you able to resolve the crisis, if at all?

Learning Activity

Read appendix B, "Discipline Guidelines for Teenagers," on page 75 of *10 Best Parenting Ways to Ruin Your Teenager.* Ask class members to form pairs. In pairs, choose one of the guidelines and

1. share about how consistently you practice it in your relationship with your teenager.

2. give an example of what the guideline looks like (or does not look like) in your home.

3. write two or three derivative "rules" based on the guideline that you would like to implement in your home.

Going Deeper

Review the rules that you have in your home regarding your teenager and his or her activities, relationships, responsibilities, and expectations. Be sure to consider unspoken rules and rules based on assumptions. Consider which rules may be outdated and in need of revision. Talk with your teenager about new rules that you can negotiate together to help make expectations clearer and life together smoother.

Reflecting on Sample Sessions

Now that you have read this example of a dialogical learning book study, let's review the particular components that make it dialogical as opposed to didactic. First, notice that before even starting the lesson, group members are provided with an orientation for an effective learning experience by teaching them how to be good group members. The group leader-teacher serves as group process facilitator, and it is the group members who carry the lesson through their participation in the group learning process.

Second, note that the session learning objectives are clearly stated at the beginning of the session (because this lesson is written for laypersons, rather than teachers, the learning objectives are written in nontechnical language as "Insights for This Session").

Third, note that the length of the session (60 to 90 minutes) accommodates expansive time for dialogue around three questions. The questions address the three categories of dialogical questions: *insight, understanding,* and *application.* Notice also that the types of questions asked in this session focus heavily on the experiential since it is assumed that the participants have read the content in the corresponding book chapter. There is no "lecture" or talk by the group leader-teacher.

Fourth, the learning activities in this session include a metaphor exercise, a powerful method that facilitates higher-order imaginative thinking. The session also has two application learning activities (one done in the group setting and the "Going Deeper," which is done at home). Both application activities are directly related to the learning objectives. Consider the following questions before moving on to chapter 8.

- Have you ever participated in a lesson that was structured like this? If so, describe that experience. Recall what you learned and how you learned it.

- Imagine yourself as a group member in the above study. How do you think you would feel sharing the answers to the discussion questions? What would the experience of the learning activities do for you?

- What do you think a group leader or teacher needs to be able to understand to lead a session like this? Do you think you are able to lead a lesson like this? Why or why not?

- Do you think a lesson format like this can work in your church? Why or why not?

CHAPTER 8

Leading a Dialogical Learning Bible Study

If you have read this far and have been paying attention, then you have learned enough about the dialogical learning approach to the small group method to be able to begin using this powerful way of learning. You have learned that dialogical learning is a *structured, intentional process that leads to insights and deep understanding and, ultimately, application in the life of the learner* (chapters 1 and 2). You have attained some understanding of small group dynamics (chapter 3). You have learned about the nature of dialogical questions (chapter 4) and about the importance of developing learning objectives (chapter 5) to ensure sound and effective educational design in creating your lessons. And you have at your disposal a broad repertoire of methods you can use to guide your small group learning process (chapter 6).

Bible study has the potential of being one of the most transforming experiences we can offer in Christian education. Done at its best, a regular small group Bible study will allow those who participate to share life at deeper levels. The focus of group dialogical Bible study is on hearing God's message to us today by allowing the Word

> ## The Role of the Group Facilitator
>
> - Clarify learning objectives.
>
> - Provide dialogical questions.
>
> - Manage the group process.

of God to speak to us through theological reflection on our lives and by learning from each other as we share insight, understanding, and experiences.

One of the problems faced by Bible study groups is that a group's effectiveness often depends on the skill and experience of one or two key people. Often that person is the "teacher," which makes everyone else perpetual "students." Sometimes one or two people dominate the discussion while others remain silent. All too often little effort is made to bridge the meaning of the text to the life experiences of the learners, which results in learners making no application of the message of God to their lives. Or worse, the Bible teacher concludes the lesson by *telling* the learners what the Bible text *should* mean for them.

In this chapter, you will learn some important things you need to know about leading a small group Bible study and review a model of dialogical learning Bible study for the small group context.[1] Remember that the dialogical learning approach is intended to result in insight, understanding, and application. In the small group, this is accomplished by facilitating a process of group theological reflection on both the text and the life experiences of the group participants. You, the group facilitator, help make this happen by (1) clarifying the learning objectives, (2) providing effective dialogical questions for the group to work through, and (3) managing the group process.

The best way to learn how to lead an effective small group dialogical learning process is to observe someone doing it well and then do it yourself. It has been said that you "can't learn it from a book." There is some truth to that statement, but it is also true that we can learn *some* things from a book. The hope is that from this book you will gain knowledge of some of the things you will need to be an effective teacher-facilitator and then really learn it by *doing* it. The reading can provide insight through understanding—the application is up to you.

Some Important Things

BASIC TECHNIQUES OF DIALOGICAL BIBLE STUDY

Theological reflection is best learned, and done, in the process of dialogue. Engaging in dialogue enables the group members to accept responsibility for their own thoughts, challenge new ideas, discern the worth and validity of current beliefs, rethink established ideas, ask deeper questions, and reflect on their own thinking process. Dialogue is a process, and the effective dialogical group leader knows how to facilitate that process. Here are some techniques to keep in mind that will allow you to help good dialogue happen in your group:

Ask a lot of open-ended questions. Provide on handouts questions that don't have right or wrong or yes or no answers.

Allow time for learners' responses. Good dialogical questions require "deep thinking," so give learners plenty of time to compose their thoughts.

Keep the dialogue going by asking follow-up questions, such as, "Let me hear more about that." "How did you know that?" "How do you think another person would respond to that?" "Can you give me an example?" "Who else has had a similar experience?" and "Does anyone have a different view on that?"

Avoid evaluating a learner's responses that may be "wrong" or off the mark, but don't ignore them either. Instead, reply to their responses as part of the dialogue with questions, such as, "Does everyone agree with that completely?" "Can anyone think of how someone might challenge that thought?" or "Are there other thoughts from the group?" Or you might merely acknowledge the response by saying, "Uh-huh," or "Thank you."

Challenge in-group speech or "Christianese," which are often merely shortcuts for not thinking. Whenever one of my students uses "Christianese," such as, "I have Jesus in my heart" or "The Lord spoke to me and said. . . ," I challenge him or her to critically think about what he or she means by asking, "And what exactly do you mean when you say that?"

Encourage guesses and hunches. Dialogue is not a linear process. Often we need to tap into people's intuition to help them arrive at insight. When you see a group member looking stumped or being timid

A Summary of Basic Techniques

- **Ask open-ended questions.**
- **Allow time for response.**
- **Ask follow-up questions.**
- **Avoid evaluating responses.**
- **Challenge "Christianese."**
- **Encourage guesses and hunches.**
- **Encourage questions from the group members.**

because he or she does not know "the right answer," ask questions that tap the imagination, such as, "What do you think *might* be an answer to that?" or "What's your hunch about that?"

Encourage questions from the group members. Good dialogue encourages your group members to ask their own questions of you and of the rest of the group. Remember that in the study group context, all members are co-teachers as well as co-learners.

Effective Use of Desists

As a child, one of my all-time favorite cartoons was Quick Draw McGraw and his faithful companion, Baba Looey (does that date me?). Quick Draw was the noble but naïve, quick-on-the-trigger sheriff who fought off wicked desperados who inevitably found their way into his quiet prairie town. Baba Looey was the devoted and wise Mexican companion who always saved Quick Draw from his misguided attempts. (In case you don't know, Quick Draw was a horse, and Baba Looey was a burro—they were the Don Quixote and Sancho Panza of Saturday mornings.) Sheriff Quick Draw's first attempt at stopping a criminal type was to cry out, "Cease and desist!" Of course, it never worked. What hardened criminal would desist bad behavior just because someone told them to?

This brings up the question, when learners "misbehave" (get off track, off subject, or become distractive to the group), how do you get them to desist without feeling like you have to pull out a Colt .44 and fire a round into the ceiling? Fortunately, there are effective ways for a teacher to say, "Cease and desist," to stop off-task behavior and get learning back on track. A group leader who knows how to stop disruptions before they spread not only stops the deviancy but at the same time has a positive effect on other learners in the group.

A *desist* is an action the group facilitator makes to stop off-task learner behavior. The trick is to use desists that not only stop unwanted behavior but that also do not distract the other learners in the group or cause undo anxiety. For example, if a group facilitator uses angry, punitive desists, then the acting-out group member may stop his or her misconduct, but the ripple effect on the other learners in the group will mean an increase in emotional anxiety and disruptive behavior. When anxiety increases, learning decreases. The quality of a desist has five indicators: *clarity, roughness, task-force, major deviance,* and *correct target.*

Clarity of desist refers to behavior by the leader that specifies who the acting-out learner is, what he or she is doing wrong, and why this is improper behavior or what the proper behavior is. ("Tom, please do not interrupt others before they are finished sharing. We want to hear what everyone has to say. And I'd like to hear your thoughts, too, when she is done.")

Roughness of desist is when the leader's attempts to stop misbehavior are expressed as impatience and anger or when the leader's facial or bodily behavior expresses anger. (The group leader slams a book against the chair and yells, "Will you three stop talking and focus on the work? You're distracting everybody!") Learners who witness a punitive or angry desist tend to respond with more behavior disruption than when they observe a desist without roughness.

Task-force desist refers to ways leaders can direct group members to the task at hand as the desist is given. For example, you witness two distracted group members who are whispering and talking to each other instead of paying attention to a group member who is providing background information on the text. You walk quietly to the learners and hand them a copy of the handout that the group is working on without commenting and without interrupting the presenter's talk.

Major deviance desist is a behavior in which the group leader selects the major disruption amid two or more deviancies that occur simultaneously. (The leader observes that one member of the group is reading a piece of paper unrelated to the lesson and also observes that two members of the group are loudly talking with each other and not engaging in the dialogue. The leader addresses the two and says, "Let's save our private conversations for later, please. We need for each member of the group to participate." As a result, the two persons stop talking and refocus, and the distracted member, overhearing the desist, puts away the paper and focuses on the discussion.)

Correct target desist means the leader desists the group member who caused the disruption, not a bystander. Few things can make a learner "tune out" quicker than to get the fallout consequence for something he or she did not do. This desist requires that the group leader practice "with-it-ness," the ability to be aware of everything that is going on in the learning environment and in the group process.

Learning effective desist techniques is one of the most valuable skills a group leader can master to help facilitate good group process. A leader who can minimize time spent on group behavior management will increase the time the group has for actual learning and sharing.[2] So it will be helpful to keep in mind the following general principles on the use of desists:

1. Soft reprimands are more effective in controlling disruptive behavior than loud reprimands.

2. When soft reprimands are used, fewer are needed.

3. Task-focused desists have more favorable ripple effects on overall group conduct than does addressing a behavior without directing the offender to the task at hand.

4. When a simple nonintrusive or nondisruptive reprimand is observed, group members tend to feel that the leader is fair and able to maintain control.

DEALING WITH THE OVERTALKER

"Overtalkers" are group members who seem to love the sound of their own voices. Often they are the first to respond to a question, and often they do so without taking the time to think about it. Many are extroverted types who need to talk to "gain an insight," but in the process tend to dominate the dialogue. Overtalkers can ruin the dialogical learning experience by monopolizing time and alienating group members. There are basically two reasons for overtalking behavior: either the overtalker is clueless about how his or her behavior is affecting the group, or the overtalker knows what he or she is doing and is deliberately sabotaging the learning process.

Either way, the most helpful approach on the part of the group leader (and the group members themselves) is to deal with the problem directly. While a clueless overtalker may initially be embarrassed at having this detrimental behavior pointed out, ultimately he or she will be appreciative. If the overtalker is being willful about disrupting the group process, that is plainly irresponsible behavior and should be dealt with as such. In his book *Seven Myths about Small Groups,* Dan Williams gives some good advice about dealing with overtalkers:

- Remind the overtalker about ground rules, such as, "Listen to one another."

- Be directive and say, "I want everyone to answer this one."

- Interrupt the person in the middle of a long speech and say, "You have made several excellent points—let's see if there is any response to what you have said."

- Stop looking at the person while he or she is talking—it usually will slow the person down.

- Solicit the help of the mature group to do the work for you, with members humorously and gently reminding the talkative person that he or she is "doing it again." (When trust has been built, such communication is possible.)

- Ask the person privately or publicly to be quiet.[3]

The Dialogical Bible Study Illustrated

The dialogical learning approach to small group Bible study allows for all group members to take part in the teaching-learning process while respecting the biblical text. The group facilitator will help the process along but will not dominate the group. The method can easily be adapted to your learners' needs and to your own teaching strengths. Additionally, you can modify the time frame as needed; however, remember that dialogue and group process takes a lot of time. While you can use the dialogical method in a typical 45-minute Sunday school time, for instance, and there is no reason why you should not do so, the ideal time needed for discussion means that you will be challenged to cut back on "lecture" time. For the typical Sunday school time frame, you may need to organize class time something like this:

Welcome and introduction (5–7 minutes)

Background orientation (7–10 minutes)

Dialogical small groups (30 minutes)

Closure (5 minutes)

That's a pretty tight schedule for most Sunday school classes, but it is doable if your class makes a commitment to it. The following illustration assumes a context other than the usual Sunday school hour, one with more expansive time for a small group dialogical learning Bible study.

Outline for Bible Study

1. Silence and centering prayer
2. First reading of the text
3. Orientation to the text
4. Second reading of the text
5. Dialogical learning experience
6. Break and fellowship
7. Sharing concerns
8. Ending the session

1. Silence and Centering Prayer

Make prayer a part of your teaching-learning experience. Begin with a period of silence and prayer. The very act of being together, waiting together in God's presence and listening for God's Word, is a significant event, so let the group experience the moment fully. Beginning with a centering prayer and meditation helps people focus on the moment. You can use various methods of prayer over the course of your meetings together. For example, guided meditative prayer is especially helpful to those new persons in the group who have little experience in prayer. This method has the advantage of helping to focus prayer in specific directions that relate to your lesson. There are many ways to lead a guided prayer. One way is to choose certain areas of focus (praise, concerns for others, concerns for self, life choices, life transitions, family, forgiveness, temptations) and prompt the class to pray for that concern in silence or with sentence prayers. Give them a few moments, then move on to the next prayer concern focus.

We learn best by doing and observing. That's just as true about prayer as any other area of life. Give your group members a chance to "learn prayer" by doing it and observing it done in your group. Other methods of prayer suitable to start your group study are the collect and litany prayers. Litanies are highly participatory prayers. The simplest way to use litanies is in responsive reading, but you can divide your class into two or three response groups, or you can incorporate individual responses as part of the litany. Some psalms lend themselves to use as litanies, for example, Psalm 100.

Do not rush this important first step. Start your group off from the very beginning of their formation with one minute of silent prayer. While it may feel uncomfortably long for most of the group, keep at it. Stay with the one minute of silence for a few sessions, then gradually begin to work your way to a five-minute time of silence. It will not take long to get there, and group members will quickly grow in their appreciation of it.

2. First Reading of the Text

Before you begin the first reading of the text, share with the group the learning objective for the session. Sharing the objective up front helps participants know where the session is headed and will help answer the "So what?" question early. Refer to chapter 5 when preparing your objectives, and remember the advice given by educator Findley Edge, who said that a good teaching objective should be brief enough to be remembered, clear enough to be written down, and specific enough to be achieved.[4]

Be sure each group member has a Bible, then read the study passage. Your group will eventually read this text at least twice. The emphasis of this first reading is on the text itself, the words, the literature, the written word. Use various translations if it will help get to the meaning of the text. Announce that for this reading the group is to be aware of a word, phrase, or image that especially speaks to them. After the reading, allow for a time of brief reflection, then invite members to share the word, phrase, or image that captured their attention or that they perceive as being central to the passage, but to do so without discussion or elaboration. Writing their responses on a flip chart will help the group keep the discussion focused. This process will allow group members to collectively focus on the structure and language of the text. And getting every participant to speak early in the session will serve as a way to get everyone into a participatory frame of mind.

3. Orientation to the Text

After the first reading of the text, share pertinent background information that the group will need in order to responsibly handle the meaning of the text during the discussion. Depending on the passage, this may be a lot, but more often than not, the information needed will be minimal. Focus on the Bible text, its style, literature, the context of the passage, key words and phrases, and the genre. Provide only relevant information about the historical background, information about the writer of the text, or the meaning of some special terms. This part should be kept to no more than about five to ten minutes. The goal here is to provide just enough background information to allow the members to respect the text and to engage in responsible interpretation during the dialogue.

4. Second Reading of the Text

Read the text a second time. For this reading you can use some of the methods for telling a Bible story or interpreting a passage from chapter 6 if the passage warrants it. During this reading, you want to lead the group to explore the primary meaning of the text (the author's message to the original audience) and ideas about contemporary application of the text. Therefore, ask the group to focus on two questions: (1) What is the writer saying to the people of the time? and (2) What is the importance of this passage for us today?

This is the time to begin facilitating good group process. Use some of the methods in chapter 6 to prompt discussion and to get your group members talking (use a talking stick, play "But I'd Like Your Opinion," or go around the circle, for example). In the early stages of the group's development, you may choose to begin the sharing to model how it is done. The responses should be brief (no mini-lectures!).

5. Dialogical Learning Experience

The fifth step of the session begins the dialogical learning experience. During this time, group members continue to examine the text for personal application as they respond to the dialogical questions about insight, understanding, and application. This is the heart of the process, and you will need to allow 40 to 45 minutes of dialogue time. If your study group is large (15 people or more), then have the group form smaller dialogue groups of four or five persons—but no more than that. Distribute the handouts with the dialogical questions or display them on a focal point (chalkboard, flip chart, or PowerPoint).

Always keep in mind that in this step the group members are being challenged to make application of the message of the text to their lives. Through the dialogical questions you provide, group members are asked to reflect on the overarching questions, "How does God invite you to change?" or "What does God invite you to do through this passage?" Refer to chapter 4 when crafting your dialogical questions.

6. Break and Fellowship

Allow sufficient time for the small groups to do their work (40 to 45 minutes), then call time and regather the participants. A 10- to 15-minute break is good here. If you want, provide coffee and donuts or cookies. Allow people to relax and mingle. Your group members will use this time not only to relax and take a "brain break," but to fellowship, share, and connect with each other.

7. Sharing Concerns

Call the group members back from the break and begin the important time of sharing personal concerns, celebrations, and prayer requests. This step can take up to a half hour. If this seems excessive, remember that this is a different kind of learning experience. This is the part that facilitates learning through relationships—and relationships mediate spiritual formation. During this time, participants share hopes, struggles, dreams, temptations, ministry concerns, and life situations. This step is part of the group formation process that will allow your group to form community, build relationships, create its corporate identity, and live into its covenant. If you will allow the gift of time and space this step calls for, this may become "church" for many in the group.

8. Ending the Session

Never underestimate the importance of closure to a group learning experience. Closure is an intentional learning step and is part of the experience; therefore, treat it as such. You may close your group study time in one of several way. Here are some possibilities:

- End the learning experience with a period of silence and then conclude with the Lord's Prayer.

- Invite each member to complete one or the other or both of the following sentences: "I thank God today for . . ." or "I ask God today. . . ," then conclude with the Lord's Prayer.

- Share news, information, or announcements, then conclude with the passing of the peace after a time of prompted prayer.

- Offer a blessing or a benediction.

You can use the Bible Study planning worksheet (appendix J) to think through and plan your dialogical learning Bible study. Remember that the key to success here is thoughtful and intentional planning and facilitating good group learning process, not covering a lot of information. Allow your group members the freedom and time to be co-learners and co-teachers.

CHAPTER 9

A Dialogical Learning Topical Study Illustrated

This chapter is an example of a topical study using the dialogical learning approach in a small group. This learning experience combines topical Bible study, story, and dialogical questions to facilitate good group dialogue. This lesson uses the story method to get to the "heart" of the matter (pun intended). Through the use of story, group members are brought more quickly to the affective domain, which is the primary area being addressed in this session. This same lesson can take a different slant by using a different vehicle: a newspaper story, an article, a report, a video clip, or an image (photograph, painting, sculpture, or other artwork). Note that in this lesson there are four dialogical questions that connect the topic with experience, and there are three application steps that lead participants from their personal experience to their church experience and on to a commitment step. As always, in dialogical learning the quality of the questions is more important than the number of questions. And when you have good questions, "less is more," because they allow for expansive group dialogue.

Welcoming the Stranger
(Or, Who Belongs and Who Does Not?)

1. ORIENTATION (5–7 MINUTES)

Welcome the group members as they arrive. Be sure to distribute Bibles and have the questions handout sheet ready for distribution. Take care of any housekeeping matters at this time so you won't interrupt the learning process later. Begin with prayer to signal the beginning of class.

2. THE SCRIPTURE STUDY (10 MINUTES)

Introduce the topic for today's study: hospitality. Share with the group members the goal of today's learning session: to examine God's perspective on who belongs and to decide how each group member will respond by choosing ways to be welcoming to others.

Begin by distributing the Bibles to group members and asking for volunteers to read the verses. Encourage the rest of the class to follow the reading in their Bibles and to refer to these verses during their dialogue. As each verse is read, summarize the passage by sharing background information and by asking the group interpretive questions about what they have just read.

Acts 9:26-28: The recently converted Saul (Paul the apostle) is not welcomed by the other disciples because of his former actions. Barnabas intercedes on behalf of Saul before the apostles.

Ephesians 2:11-19: The Gentiles were once outsiders, "aliens from the commonwealth of Israel," and without hope. But through Christ, we are no longer strangers and aliens, but rather, citizens and members of the household of God.

Acts 15:7-9: Peter preaches that God makes no distinction between Jew and Gentile.

1 Corinthians 12:12-13: Paul says that all Christians are members of the body of Christ, made one through the Spirit.

3. THE STORY[1] (3 MINUTES)

Explain to the group that we will approach the topic of welcoming the stranger by listening to a short story. Invite the group members to get comfortable and to listen attentively to the story. Read "The Tree of All Hearts."

The Tree of All Hearts

The night of the big storm was over. By the light of the morning sun, Alicia Robin looked all around the courtyard. From her perch on the bench, she looked sadly to where the large oak tree that had been her home lay on its side, like a fallen skyscraper. The storm had brought the clouds and cold rain, and along with it the terrible lightning that had struck the large oak tree where Alicia and her family had lived as long as she could remember. This had been her parents' home, and their parents' home before them. The tree had been home for countless other robins as they returned year after year to build nests and start new families.

Now the old oak tree was gone, and so was Alicia's home. She gathered her family together. They all looked so frightened.

"Is our home gone, Mommy?" asked Peter Robin, the youngest.

"Are we homeless?" asked Sarah Robin.

"We don't have a place to live now, Mother!" cried Albert Robin, the oldest.

Alicia tried to look brave, though she felt a little scared too. "We'll be all right children; we'll find a new home in which to live. It will be a home of our very own."

And so the Robin family started their search for a new home, a place of their own and a place where they belonged.

They did not go far before they came across a poplar tree. "This looks like a nice place," said Sarah. "Let's live here!"

But then a puffy gray squirrel peeked out of a hole and said, "You can't live here; this tree is just for squirrels. You don't belong here! Please go away."

Feeling sad, the Robin family kept looking. Soon they came across a maple tree. "This will make a nice house," said Peter. "Let's live here!"

Just then a very serious looking owl flew down and said, "No, you can't live here. This maple tree is for owls only! You don't belong here. Please go away."

The Robin family felt hurt. "It feels sad not having a place where we belong," said Sarah. "Yes, it is sad," said Alicia Robin, "but we must keep looking. We will find a place where we belong."

And so they continued to look. Soon they came across a beautiful pear tree, with lots of branches and beautiful leaves. "This is it! I know it," cried Albert. "This is our new home!"

But just then, a small flock of sparrows fluttered around them, yelling, "No, no! This is the sparrow tree! You cannot move here. You do not belong! Please go away!"

Alicia Robin felt so sad upon hearing this that she did not know what to do. She was worried about her family and was afraid that she would never find a home for them. She tried to be brave in front of her children, but soon she began to cry.

"Why are you crying?" said a voice. Alicia, Albert, Sarah, and Peter looked, and there was a friendly raven, beautiful and black as night.

"We have lost our home," replied Alicia.

"And we don't seem to belong anywhere," said Albert.

"Nobody wants us," cried Sarah, on the verge of tears.

"I know a place where you belong," said the raven. "Come to the Tree of All Hearts. Everyone is welcomed there, and you can have a home among all of God's creatures."

The raven led Alicia and her family across the forest to a beautiful meadow. At its center was the most beautiful tree they had ever seen. It was the Tree of All Hearts. They saw other robins there, and owls and squirrels and sparrows, and all kinds of creatures. They were amazed that they seemed to live happily together: working, playing, and worshipping together.

"What is this place?" asked Alicia in wonder.

"This is the Tree of All Hearts," said the raven. "This is the Creator's special tree, where all of God's creatures are welcomed to live and work and worship together under God's rule of peace and love."

"Can we live here?" asked Albert.

"Yes, you can live here," said the raven, "You belong here if you are God's creature. All are welcomed here who love God. Welcome to your new home!"

And so Alicia Robin and her family found their new home in the Tree of All Hearts.

4. DIALOGICAL REFLECTION AND SHARING (30–40 MINUTES)

Distribute the following dialogical study questions on a handout to the group members. If the group is large, ask the class to form smaller discussion groups of four or five members, but no more than five (if two class members form a pair, invite them to join a group of three, or direct each to join a separate group). Allow the groups sufficient time to work through the questions. Call "time" about ten minutes before concluding, and direct the groups to work on the application questions.

1. Have you ever had to find a new home and a new community? What was the most difficult part of becoming part of a new community? Have you ever felt like an "outsider" who did not belong? Share that story.

2. Do you think your church does a good job of welcoming new people into community? How so?

3. Have you ever visited a place for the first time that felt like "home"? Describe it.

4. To what extent do you think God welcomes all people "home"? Are there limitations or exceptions to God's welcoming posture? Why or why not?

5. APPLICATION (10 MINUTES)

1. Share a story or describe how hospitality was practiced in your culture, your family of origin, or your current family.

2. Reflect on your experience of your church. If you were to help your church become the "Church of All Hearts," what changes would you need to make? What practices of welcoming and hospitality can you identify that you will keep?

3. Using a flip chart or the chalkboard, brainstorm with your group ways you can help make your church a more welcoming and inviting church. When you have completed the list, state which one you are committed to practicing in the next month.

6. CONCLUSION (5 MINUTES)

Call the groups back when it is time to conclude the study. Ask individual group members to share what they committed to for helping the church be more welcoming and inviting to strangers. Remind the group that the goal of learning is to actually practice what is learned. Stress that in the Christian life, the purpose of learning is for obedience. End the session in prayer, asking God to help you be obedient in welcoming the stranger and welcoming all in God's name.

Appendices

APPENDIX A
Basic Bible Quiz

Directions: This quiz tests your basic Bible knowledge. Answer each question to the best of your ability. If the group leader allows, you can work on this quiz with a partner.

1. How many books are there in the Old Testament?
   __ A. 39   __ C. 55
   __ B. 40   __ D. 66

2. How many books are there in the New Testament?
   __ A. 24   __ C. 35
   __ B. 27   __ D. 37

3. Who is the traditional author of the Gospel of John?
   __ A. John the Baptist
   __ B. John, son of Zebedee
   __ C. John of Arimathea
   __ D. The Beloved Disciple

4. Which was the first Gospel to be written?
   __ A. Matthew   __ C. Luke
   __ B. Mark   __ D. John

5. Which of the following is not a synoptic Gospel?
   __ A. Matthew   __ C. Luke
   __ B. Mark   __ D. John

6. The New Testament was written only by the original disciples of Jesus.
   __ True   __ False

7. What is the name of the last book in the Old Testament?
   _____

8. When was the first Gospel written?
___ A. AD 7   ___ C. AD 65
___ B. AD 35   ___ D. AD 70

9. Which parable is not found in the Gospel of John?
___ A. The Lost Coin
___ B. The Prodigal Son
___ C. The Ten Virgins
___ D. The Lost Sheep
___ E. All of the above

10. Which New Testament book was written first?
___ A. Matthew
___ B. First Thessalonians
___ C. First Peter
___ D. First Corinthians

11. Place these Old Testament Kings in order:
___ A. David   ___ C. Solomon
___ B. Josiah   ___ D. Saul

12. Where are the "I am" sayings of Jesus found?
___ A. Matthew and Mark
___ B. Only in Luke
___ C. Luke and Matthew
___ D. Only in John

13. Number these in chronological order
___ Moses   ___ Noah
___ Abraham   ___ Ezekiel
___ David

14. In what year was Jesus born?
___ A. The year 0
___ B. 5 BC
___ C. AD 5
___ D. None of the above

15. How long was Jesus' earthly ministry?
    __ A. 1 year   __ C. 3 years
    __ B. 2 years   __ D. 4 years

16. In which Gospel is found the story of Jesus' ascension into heaven?
    __ A. The Gospels of Matthew and Mark
    __ B. The Gospel of John
    __ C. The Gospel of Luke only
    __ D. The Gospel of Thomas
    __ E. None of the above

17. There are only four Gospels in existence.
    __ True   __ False

18. Which of the following are mentioned *only* in the Gospel of John?
    __ A. The "I am" sayings of Jesus
    __ B. The water turned to wine
    __ C. The Samaritan woman
    __ D. The resurrection of Lazarus
    __ E. The washing of the disciples' feet
    __ F. Jesus' last prayer

19. How many missionary journeys did Paul make?
    __ A. 1   __ C. 3
    __ B. 2   __ D. 4

20. Which prophet ministered to the people of Israel during their exile?
    __ A. Amos   __ D. Ezekiel
    __ B. Habakkuk   __ E. Jonah
    __ C. Zechariah

Answers to the Basic Bible Quiz

1. A. 39

2. B. 27

3. The answer can be B. John, son of Zebedee or D. The Beloved Disciple. Strictly speaking, the answer is D, since the author is identified as such in the Gospel.

4. B. Mark. Mark's Gospel was the earliest of the Gospels in the canon and was written around AD 65.

5. D. John. The Gospel of John is not a synoptic Gospel, that is, the lens through which it views Jesus is different from the other three Gospels.

6. The answer is False. Luke and Paul, who wrote major portions of the New Testament, were not original disciples of Jesus during his ministry. One of the tests for inclusion in the canon of the New Testament was apostolicity, but that did not require that a disciple or apostle himself write the work.

7. Malachi

8. C. AD 65. This is the traditional date for the writing of the Gospel of Mark.

9. E. All of the above. There are no parables in the Gospel of John.

10. B. First Thessalonians. Paul's epistle to the church at Thessalonica was the first "book" in the New Testament to be written and is typically dated around AD 50 or 51.

11. (1) Saul, (2) David, (3) Solomon, (4) Josiah

12. D. Only in John

13. In chronological order: (1) Noah, (2) Abraham, (3) Moses, (4) David, (5) Ezekiel

14. B. 5 BC. Strangely enough, due to a miscalculation by the monk who gave us our modern way of counting years (the Gregorian calendar), Jesus was born in 5 BC, "Before Christ."

15. C. 3 years. But scholars have argued for anywhere from a one-year to a four-year ministry.

16. E. None of the above. The account of Jesus' ascension is found in the Book of Acts.

17. False. There are four Gospels in the canon, the "accepted books," of the New Testament, but several other Gospels are in existence, the best known of which is the Gospel of Thomas.

18. The correct answers are: A, B, C, D, E, F. All of these are mentioned only in the Gospel of John.

19. C. 3. Paul's third and final missionary journey ended in Rome, where he was martyred.

20. Ezekiel

Scoring: Give yourself 5 points for each correct answer.	
Your Score	What Your Score Means
95–100	Excellent! You should be teaching Sunday school or a Bible study group if you aren't already!
55–90	Not bad. You've been paying attention, are a good student of the Bible, and are able to recall basic information about the Bible. Good going!
25–50	You need to invest in a good study Bible!
0–20	You are new to the church, have been sleeping in class, may have gone to seminary, or have been the Sunday school superintendent or director and haven't attended a Bible study class in years.

APPENDIX B
Sample Group Covenant

Commitment to a group covenant can go a long way toward helping your group establish corporate values, articulate expectations, and hold each other accountable to making the group experience as meaningful as possible. You can use the following sample group covenant as a model for your group. Adapt the sample covenant to your needs, or create one with your group.

Make copies of the covenant for the group members and suggest that each member sign the covenant when entering the group.

Our Covenant

As members of the body of Christ seeking to learn and to grow together, we covenant with each other to

- affirm one another,
- be available and present,
- pray for each other steadfastly,
- be open and transparent,
- be honest,
- be sensitive,
- maintain confidentiality when asked.

To affirm one another means that we recognize that each of us is on the journey to growth and maturity. We will accept each member where he or she is and will not expect perfection, but rather, extend grace to each, believing that each is beloved of God.

To be available and present means that we will be good stewards of our time, beginning and ending on time, and participating fully in the process of learning together through sharing and responsible learning.

To pray for each other steadfastly means that we will intentionally pray for each member of our group when we are together and when we are apart, asking for God's redemptive presence and guidance in one another's lives.

To be open and transparent means that we will trust the group by being willing to be vulnerable in order to be challenged to grow, that we will work at being persons of integrity in our dealings and in our representations of ourselves.

To be honest means that we will speak the truth in love, share accurate information when required, and take responsibility only for our own growth and not that of another.

To be sensitive means that we will be redemptive and compassionate in our dealings with one another, even in times when challenge and admonition are appropriate postures. At all times we will strive to maintain the other persons' dignity.

To maintain confidentiality when asked means that we will honor requests to be responsible with personal and sensitive information that a group member shares as appropriate. But we covenant that we will not be bound by information that can be harmful to others if keeping a confidence means we are helpless to help or can prevent a harm.

APPENDIX C
Group Math

Small Group Size	Best for
Dyad (2 persons)	Good for intimate sharing and for efficient processing of simple concepts or personal experiences that do not need to be shared with the larger group as a whole.
Triad (3 persons)	Good for discussion but has drawbacks and limitations. For example, a "two-against-one" dynamic might develop, or two dominant members might shut out a passive member.
4 persons	Optimum for a discussion question dialogue. Can effectively handle up to five questions in an allotted time of about 40 to 45 minutes.
5 persons	Good for a discussion question and dialogue. Can effectively handle three to four questions in an allotted time of about 40 to 45 minutes.
9 persons	The optimum group for a problem-solving task. This size group will come up with just about every possible solution to a problem without getting stuck.
15 persons	Optimum for a small study group. This size group can remain intimate and interactive with enough space and time and with a good teacher-facilitator. It can also form smaller units (dyad or triad or a group of 4 or 5) for more effective discussion followed by debriefing.
18 persons	Optimum for a traditional class as it is still small enough to be intimate, though cohesion starts to become a challenge. A good group teacher-leader can facilitate dialogical learning by forming smaller units for learning (dyad, triad, or a group of 4 or 5).
25 persons	Ideal for classroom instruction and maximum for a "small group." A good teacher-facilitator will need to work intentionally and consistently to overcome the logistics of this larger group. Dialogical learning becomes difficult at this size without consistently regrouping into smaller discussion groups.

How to Deal with Learners' Responses

1. Demonstrate that the responses are valued by:
   - repeating the response
   - encouraging creative responses
   - writing responses on the board
   - referring back to the response at a later time

2. Clarify responses by:
   - paraphrasing responses
   - helping the learner modify a response for accuracy or clarification
   - asking the learner to give an example
   - asking, "Can you say that in a different way?"

3. Relate and extend response by:
   - using the response as an example or as an explanation of an idea
   - using the response as a contrast to a previous response

4. Summarize with a response by:
   - using it to make a point
   - using it to draw a conclusion
   - using it to recap the concept being learned

5. Deal with incorrect responses by:
   - rephrasing the question with, "If I were to say . . ."
   - saying, "I'm not sure what you mean by that."
   - asking, "Can you say that in a different way?"
   - saying, "That's an interesting answer. I've never thought of it that way before!"

A Dialogical Questions Taxonomy

A taxonomy categorizes and describes levels of learning from lower to higher and from simple to complex.

Category of Dialogical Question	Definition	Intent of Question	Types of Questions
Insight	*Insight* means to understand the inner nature of oneself and of one's relationship with God and others.	*Questions of insight* help learners uncover knowledge of their inner selves and of their relationships.	Affective Questions • Empathy • Values • Opinions • Self-Awareness Experiential Questions • Past • Present • Future
Understanding	*Understanding* means to know what you know and why it is so.	*Questions of understanding* help learners critically know what they know (concepts, facts, prejudices) and why it is so, and to uncover what they do not know.	Cognitive Questions • Concepts • Explanation • Analysis • Interpretation
Application	*Application* means to be able to use what you know in a variety of contexts and situations.	*Questions of application* help the learners to use what they know in their various life situations and contexts.	Behavioral Questions • Practices • Skills • Habits • Actions Volitional Questions • Choosing • Committing • Valuing

APPENDIX F
How to Write a Case Study

Writing a good case study involves following certain rules and conventions. A good case study is a hybrid composed of journalistic, artistic, and literary approaches. You will need to adhere to some of the guidelines of good journalism (answering who, what, when, where, how, and why). Unbiased reporting of the facts, with a high degree of accuracy, is one goal to keep in mind. Cases, unlike articles and essays, avoid arguments of opinion or hypothesis. The temptation to editorialize with statements such as, "It was a typical board meeting," or "Mr. Johnson exercised brilliant leadership," should be resisted. More appropriate are comments such as, "Members of the board reported that their meeting was a typical one," or "Mr. Johnson was acknowledged by the congregation to have provided them with brilliant leadership."

In general, state things that are to be taken as unalterable facts, while reserving statements of opinion for the persons or groups who hold them. For small group dialogical learning situations, you should try to keep your case study to one page. Use the following outline as a guide to writing your case study:

1. *Introduction.* A statement of the problem or scenario and a hint at various alternatives that the protagonist(s) is/are considering. Placing a concrete setting at the beginning of a case is a good technique to get the reader immediately involved in the action and orients the reader to the case.

2. *Exposition.* Several paragraphs of background material serve to give the readers essential facts about the past and lead them to the present.

3. *Development section.* The central issues unfold in this part of the case. Included in this section are conversations among participants, reflections they make, and other significant contemporary data.

4. *Summary.* This section offers a recapitulation of the problem.

5. *Dialogical learning questions.* Provide opening dialogical learning questions to help the group start its work.

6. *Exhibits.* In more complex and detailed cases, any pertinent material that would detract from the text by introducing an element of artificiality can be included in an appendix.

A Sample Case Study

The Recalcitrant Maintenance Supervisor

Jim came onto the ministerial staff of the Central Community Church as an educational director. At his first staff meeting with the senior minister and the other staff members, Jim was delegated responsibility for supervision of the buildings and grounds staff. He was brought up to date on what was obviously a very frustrating, long-standing situation with the church staff and some members.

Jim was informed that the building and grounds supervisor, Greg, was a source of great frustration. He often missed assignments, made decisions on his own without consulting staff, and often did not return calls from staff or other church members. Since he worked as a firefighter, Greg was often unavailable for several days at a time, including some weekends, when many church activities, weddings, and community events at the church buildings took place. His communication with other part-time maintenance staff was sporadic, unclear, and sometimes nonexistent.

As the "rest of the story" unfolded, Jim could feel his anxiety rising. He was told that Greg was a longtime member of the church, and his extended family was very active and "influential" in the church (his wife was an employee of the church daycare center, served on several church committees, and taught Sunday school; his sister served on the church's Christian education committee). Furthermore, Greg had held the position of building and grounds supervisor at the church before but had been dismissed for the same behaviors that were now frustrating the staff and church members. The senior pastor had hired him back during a time when Greg was having financial difficulties.

Jim was told that his responsibility was to supervise Greg and to see that Greg did his job. The senior minister "hinted" strongly that if Jim could not help Greg get his act together and do his job, he would support Jim if it became necessary to "dismiss" Greg as supervisor.

Exploratory Questions:

- How do you think Jim felt after leaving his first staff meeting?
- Identify the emotional-relational triangles in this situation.
- Identify the key issue(s) you see in this situation.
- Have you ever experienced a similar situation as described here? Tell that story.
- How would you advise Jim to proceed?
- How would you advise Jim to proceed from a biblical point of view?
- Is there a biblical metaphor or story you can offer to Jim that can provide a theological frame of reference for thinking about his situation?

APPENDIX H
Role of the Group Facilitator

Making the switch from "teacher" to group facilitator can be a challenge. Here is a handy reminder checklist of the roles of a good group facilitator.

☐ Pray for your group and its individual members.

☐ Prepare.
  ○ Prepare the meeting space: the learning environment can facilitate or hinder good group learning process.
  ○ Prepare yourself: you will only be able to be a resource to the group to the extent that you yourself are prepared and ready.

☐ Set the tone.
  ○ Model openness.
  ○ Model enthusiasm.
  ○ Model accountability.

☐ Help establish group values and norms:
  ○ Trust
  ○ Unity
  ○ Purposeful learning
  ○ The group covenant

☐ Give instructions.
  ○ Never invite a group into a vacuum.
  ○ Provide clear directions for learning activities.
  ○ Provide clear instructions for group process.

☐ Guide the dialogical learning process.
  ○ Begin and end on time.
  ○ Walk around and monitor discussions.
  ○ Watch for "sick" or "stuck" groups.
  ○ Provide clarification when needed.
  ○ Provide intervention when needed.

☐ Resource.
  ○ Provide materials.
  ○ Provide for general group administrative needs.
  ○ Train the subgroup leaders.
  ○ Train and support the members.

☐ Encourage.
  ○ Encourage healthy dialogue.
  ○ Encourage good group member roles.
  ○ Encourage growth.
  ○ Encourage challenge.

☐ Provide healthy closure.
  ○ Be highly visible during closure.
  ○ Provide for dissolution processes.
  ○ Extend overt invitation for recommitment if appropriate.
  ○ Allow for expressions of celebration and grief.

APPENDIX I
Experiential Questions Categories

Experiential questions facilitate the dialogical learning process by tapping into the learner's memories and experiences in order to connect to truth and insight in a way that leads to application. Remember that it is only when a learner connects personal life experience to truth that meaningful learning occurs.

Body
- an accident
- an illness
- awareness
- broken bones
- bruises
- changes
- type

Church
- a crisis
- a worship experience
- favorite pastor
- favorite teacher
- first memory
- home church
- most memorable sermon
- smells, feelings, sounds

Faith
- awareness
- challenge to
- changes in
- commitment

- conversion experience
- doubt
- growth in
- religious experience
- repentance

Family
- birth order
- birthdays
- crises
- deaths and funerals
- extended family
- family reunions
- favorite aunt/uncle
- first memory
- leaving home
- migrations
- moves to new home
- name(s)
- parents
- relationships in
- rituals and practices
- siblings
- vacations

Feelings
anxiety, peaceful
brave, afraid
competent, inadequate
energized, tired
enthusiasm, skeptical
fear, courage
glad, angry
grateful, jealous
grief and mourning
happy, unhappy
hope, despair
joy, depressed
lonely, loved
sad, sorrowful
strong, weak

Life Events and Transitions
births
college
deaths
divorces
first car
first date
first day of school
first girlfriend/boyfriend
first job

friendships
leaving home
leavings, separations
marriages
moves
new beginnings
parenting
retirement
returning home

Vocation
first job
worst job
best job
last job
dream job
career choice
finding a job
losing a job
getting fired
being a boss
calling
competence
coworkers
money
salary
first paycheck

Bible Study Planning Sheet

---

1. Silence and centering prayer

---

2. First reading of the text

   Study text:

   Learning objectives for this session:

---

3. Orientation to the text

   Basic background:

   Author and audience:

   Literary type:

   Key terms and phrases:

   Historical context:

   Other:

---

4. Second reading of the text

   Reading method to use:

---

5. Dialogical learning questions

   Ask experiential questions (past, present, future)

   Insight:

   Understanding:

   Application:

   Affective:

   Cognitive:

   Behavioral:

   Volitional:

---

6. Break and fellowship

---

7. Sharing concerns

---

8. Ending the session

Characteristics of a Good Group Member

Good group learning experiences do not happen naturally; they are a result of intentional and responsible behaviors by group members. So, remember that a good group must be taught and trained to be a good group, and that is the job of the group leader or facilitator.

You can create and use a handout similar to the one on the following page to orient and remind your participants about how to be good group members. A handout with information like this one can be very helpful in the initial orientation meetings for establishing norms and values.

How to Be a Good Group Member

A good group depends on the good will and participation of its members. Remember, a group is only as good as its weakest member—don't be that person in your group! Below are the characteristics of a good group member.

A good group member . . .

- comes to meetings on time
- supports the work of the group
- shares ideas
- takes responsibilities for duties assigned
- believes in the significance of the work
- communicates honestly
- demonstrates accountability
- recognizes his or her strengths and limitations
- determines to be honest and transparent with others in the group
- participates in dialogue and discussion
- takes time to think
- listens to what other members say
- gives reasons for his or her answers
- stays on the task or on the topic under discussion
- allows himself or herself to be challenged in order to grow
- can negotiate the level of confidentiality he or she needs
- asks thought-provoking questions
- asks for others' opinions
- asks, "How does this apply to me?"
- asks, "What am I learning?"

NOTES

Introduction

1. Roberta Hestenes, *Using the Bible in Groups* (Philadelphia: Westminster, 1983), 21.

2. Israel Galindo, *The Craft of Christian Teaching: Essentials for Becoming a Very Good Teacher* (Valley Forge, PA: Judson Press, 1998), 137.

3. Ibid., 138.

4. Ibid., 138–39.

Chapter 1

1. http://divorcereform.org/mel/rbaptisthigh.html, The Associated Press, accessed 12/30/99.

2. Morton Kelsey and Harold Burgess, eds., *Can Christians Be Educated?* (Birmingham, AL: Religious Education Press, 1977), 7.

3. Peter L. Benson and Carolyn H. Eklyn, *Effective Christian Education: A National Study of Protestant Congregations: A Summary Report on Faith, Loyalty, and Congregational Life* (Minneapolis: Search Institute, 1999), 2.

4. Malcom Knowles, *The Modern Practice of Adult Education* (New York: Association Press, 1971). See also Leon McKenzie, *The Religious Education of Adults* (Birmingham, AL: Religious Education Press, 1982).

Chapter 2

1. William Faulkner, who, like Carl Rogers, did say that you can't teach anyone anything, has echoed this thought. And Galileo said, "You cannot teach a man anything; you can only help him find it within himself." Dialogical learning may be the key to helping people think and learn and find the answers to important questions within themselves.

2. The categories of knowledge, comprehension, application, analysis, synthesis, and evaluation, and those of the affective list (receiving, responding, valuing, organization and characterization) are taxonomies of learning.

A taxonomy categorizes and describes these levels of learning from lower to higher and from simple to complex. To learn more about taxonomies of learning, perform an Internet search on the term "learning taxonomy." You will come across more information than you likely can use on the topic.

3. According to a study by John and Sylvia Ronsvalle of The Empty Tomb (a Christian service and research organization based in Illinois that examines giving trends and church priorities, www.emptytomb.org), in 2003 members of Christian churches in the United States gave an average of less than 2.6 percent of their income to churches. But that figure ranges between 2.2 and 2.9 percent in various studies. Regardless, those figures are a far cry from the proverbial tithe (10 percent).

4. See Israel Galindo, *The Craft of Christian Teaching: Essentials for Becoming a Very Good Teacher* (Valley Forge, PA: Judson Press, 1998), 14–18.

5. Henri J. M. Nouwen, *Creative Ministry* (Garden City, NY: Doubleday, 1971), 4 (emphasis added).

6. E. Glenn Hinson, "Recovering the Pastor's Role as Spiritual Guide," in *Spiritual Dimensions of Pastoral Care,* ed. G. L. Borchert and A. D. Lester (Philadelphia: Westminster, 1985), 26–27.

7. Morton Kelsey and Harold Burgess, *Can Christians Be Educated?* (Birmingham, AL: Religious Education Press, 1977), 7.

8. See note 3 above.

9. Albert J. Wollen, *Miracles Happen in Group Bible Study* (Glendale, CA: Regal, 1976), 71.

Chapter 3

1. See David Bohm, *On Dialogue* (New York: Brunner-Routledge, 1996), for a more comprehensive treatment on the nature of dialogue.

2. The number of motivations for joining a group may be as varied as the number of people who make up the group and can include wanting to have a sense of being a part of something, seeking a feeling of being wanted, wanting an opportunity to work with others, wanting to learn, needing a chance to give of oneself, or wanting a chance to use skills and talent.

3. Roberta Hestenes, *Using the Bible in Groups* (Philadelphia: Westminster, 1983), 21. See appendix H, "Role of the Group Facilitator."

4. See appendix B for a sample group covenant.

5. See appendix K for "Characteristics of a Good Group Member." You can use this information to train your group members during the norming and forming stage of its development.

6. Marvin E. Shaw, *Group Dynamics: The Psychology of Small Group Behavior,* 3rd ed. (New York: McGraw-Hill, 1981), 169.

Chapter 4

1. Grant P. Wiggins and Jay McTighe rightly point out that understanding is not a single concept but, rather, a family of interrelated abilities. In their schema, understanding has six facets: explanation, interpretation, perspective, application, empathy, and self-understanding. They have provided an elegant and useful nonhierarchical and integrated taxonomy of learning in their book, *Understanding by Design* (Alexandria, VA: Association for Supervision and Curriculum Development, 1998).

2. See appendix E for a summary chart of the three categories of dialogical questions and the corresponding types of questions.

3. Roberta Hestenes, *Using the Bible in Groups* (Philadelphia: Westminster, 1983), 102. Hestenes has a wonderful listing of dialogical questions relating to past, present, and future experiences on pages 102–4. Additionally, she offers different types of what she terms "sharing questions" that are applicable to the small group dialogical learning approach.

Chapter 6

1. This material is taken from Israel Galindo, *The Craft of Christian Teaching: Essentials for Becoming a Very Good Teacher* (Valley Forge, PA: Judson Press, 1998), 140–41. Used with permission of the publisher.

2. For a collection of short stories and parables you can use in this way, see Israel Galindo and Alexander O. Gonzalez, *The Tree of all Hearts: Modern Parables for Teaching Faith* (Macon, GA: Smyth & Helwys, 2001).

3. In Howard Gardner, *Frames of Mind: The Theory of Multiple Intelligences* (New York: Basic Books, 1983). Gardner identifies eight different intelligences, of which music is one.

Chapter 8

1. There are several models you can use for the dialogical learning method. For additional models that you can use or adapt, see Roberta Hestenes, *Using the Bible in Groups* (Philadelphia: Westminster, 1983), in which she introduces additional methods that are suitable for dialogical learning. See also Walter Wink, *Transforming Bible Study: A Leader's Guide* (Nashville: Abingdon, 1989) for another model of Bible study that facilitates dialogical learning; and

Paul Clasper, "Base Community Method of Bible Study," in *Church Educator*, July 1993, for a shared teaching-learning approach similar to the example given in this chapter.

2. W. C. Becker et al., "Production and Elimination of Disruptive Classroom Behavior by Systematically Varying Teachers' Behavior," *Journal of Applied Behavior Analysis*, (1968) 1:35–45; W. R. Borg et al., "Teacher Classroom Management Skills and Pupil Behavior," *Journal of Experimental Education*, (1975) 44:52–58; E. T. Emmer et al., "Effective Classroom Management at the Beginning of the School Year," *Elementary School Journal* (1980) 80: 219–31; J. S. Kounin, *Discipline and Group Management in Classrooms* (New York: Holt, Rinehart and Winston, 1970).

3. Dan Williams, *Seven Myths about Small Groups* (Downers Grove: InterVarsity Press, 1991), 127–28.

4. Findley Edge, *Teaching for Results* (Nashville: Broadman & Holman, 1999).

Chapter 9

1. This story is from Israel Galindo and Alexander O. Gonzalez, *The Tree of All Hearts: Modern Parables for Teaching Faith* (Macon, GA: Smyth & Helwys, 2001). Used with permission of the publisher.

BIBLIOGRAPHY

Arnold, Jeffrey. *The Big Book on Small Groups.* Downers Grove, IL: InterVarsity Press, 2004.

Becker, W.C., et al. "Production and Elimination of Disruptive Classroom Behavior by Systematically Varying Teachers' Behavior." *Journal of Applied Behavior Analysis* (1968) 1:35–45.

Beebe, Steven A. *Communication in Small Groups: Principles and Practices.* Glenview, IL: Scott, Foresman, 2004.

Benson, Peter L., and Carolyn H. Eklin. *Effective Christian Education: A National Study of Protestant Congregations: A Summary Report on Faith, Loyalty, and Congregational Life.* Minneapolis: Search Institute, 1990.

Bohm, D. *On Dialogue.* Edited by Lee Nichol. London: Routledge, 1997.

Borg, W. R., et al. "Teacher Classroom Management Skills and Pupil Behavior." *Journal of Experimental Education* (1975) 44:52–58.

Bormann, Ernest G., and Nancy C. Bormann. *Effective Small Group Communication.* Minneapolis: Burgess, 1971.

Braden, Suzanne G., and Shirley F. Clement. *Small Groups: Getting Started.* Discipleship Resources, 1989.

Burbules, N. *Dialogue in Teaching: Theory and Practice.* New York: Teachers College Press, 1993.

Cantor, Lee. "Be an Assertive Teacher." *Instructor,* 88, no. 60, 1978, 96–97.

Cathcart, Robert S., and Larry A. Samovar. *Small Group Communication: A Reader.* 3rd ed. Dubuque, IA: W. C. Brown, 1979.

Clasper, Paul. "Base Community Method of Bible Study." *Church Educator,* July 1993.

Edge, Findley. *Teaching for Results.* Nashville: Broadman & Holman, 1999.

Emmer, E. T., et al. "Effective Classroom Management at the Beginning of the School Year." *Elementary School Journal* (1980) 80:219–31.

Evertson, C. M., and E. Emmer. "Preventive Classroom Management," in D. L. Ducke, ed., *Helping Teachers Manage Classrooms.* Alexandria, VA: Association for Supervision and Curriculum Development, 1982.

Galindo, Israel. *A Christian Educator's Book of Lists.* Macon, GA: Smyth & Helwys, 2003.

———. *The Craft of Christian Teaching: Essentials for Becoming a Very Good Teacher.* Valley Forge, PA: Judson Press, 1998.

———. "Methods of Christian Education toward Christian Spiritual Formation," *Review & Expositor* 98, no. 3 (Summer 2001): 411–29.

———. *Myths: Fact and Fiction about Teaching and Learning.* Richmond, VA: Educational Consultants, 2005.

Galindo, Israel, and Alexander O. Gonzalez. *The Tree of All Hearts: Modern Parables for Teaching Faith.* Macon, GA: Smyth & Helwys, 2001.

Galindo, Israel, and Don Reagan. *10 Best Parenting Ways to Ruin Your Teenager.* Richmond, VA: Educational Consultants, 2005.

Gardner, Howard. *Frames of Mind: The Theory of Multiple Intelligences.* New York: Basic Books, 1983.

Goffman, E. *The Presentation of Self in Everyday Life.* London: Penguin, 1959.

Griffin, Emory A. *Getting Together: A Guide for Good Groups.* Downers Grove, IL: InterVarsity Press, 1983.

Habermas, J. *The Theory of Communicative Action.* Vol. 1. Cambridge: Polity Press, 1984.

Hestenes, Roberta. *Using the Bible in Groups.* Philadelphia: Westminster, 1983.

Hinson, E. Glenn. "Recovering the Pastor's Role as Spiritual Guide." In *Spiritual Dimensions of Pastoral Care,* ed. G. L. Borchert and A. D. Lester (Philadelphia: Wesminster, 1985).

Kouinin, Jacob. *Discipline and Group Management in Classrooms.* New York: Holt, Rinehart and Winston, 1977.

MacGregor, Jean, et al. *Strategies for Energizing Large Classes: From Small Groups to Learning Communities.* San Francisco: Jossey-Bass, 2000.

Mallison, John. *Building Small Groups in the Christian Community.* Renewal Publications, 1978.

Mercer, N. *The Guided Construction of Knowledge.* Cleveland: Multilingual Matters, 1995.

Olmstead, Michael S., and A. Paul Hare. *The Small Group.* 2nd ed. New York: Random House, 1977.

Phillips, Gerald M. *Communication and the Small Group.* 2nd ed. Indianapolis: Bobbs-Merrill, 1973.

Shaw, Marvin E. *Group Dynamics: The Psychology of Small Group Behavior.* New York: McGraw-Hill, 1976.

Vaugh, Bill. *The Dynamics of Small Groups within the Church.* Kansas City: Beacon Hill, 1980.

Wardhaugh, Ronald. *How Conversation Works.* Oxford: Blackwell, 1985.

Webber, A. "O.K. Kids, Let's Quiet Down." *Teacher Education* 13, no. 2, (N.D.), 23–32.

Williams, Dan. *Seven Myths about Small Groups.* Downers Grove, IL: InterVarsity Press, 1991.

Wink, Walter. *Transforming Bible Study: A Leader's Guide.* Nashville: Abingdon, 1989.

Wollen, Albert J. *Miracles Happen in Group Bible Study.* Glendale, CA: Regal, 1976.

Youngquist, Joanne. *Leading Small Groups into Scripture Study: Here's How.* Denver: Living the Good News, 1990.

FOR READER'S NOTES

For Reader's Notes

For Reader's Notes

elated Resources

RISTIAN EDUCATION PLANNING RESOURCES

arting Our Course: Renewing the Church's Teaching Ministry
da R. Isham   0-8170-1254-0 $11.00

bracing the Future: A Guide to Reshaping Your Church's Teaching Ministry
ited by Linda R. Isham   0-8170-1327-X $16.00

e Teaching Church at Work: A Manual for the Board of Christian Education
ited by Kenneth D. Blazier and Linda R. Isham   0-8170-1191-9 $13.00

e Work of the Sunday School Superintendent
is W. Jones; Revised by Ruth L. Spencer   0-8170-1229-X $10.00

RISTIAN EDUCATION TEACHING RESOURCES

e Craft of Christian Teaching: Essentials for Becoming a Very Good Teacher
ael Galindo   0-8170-1280-X $16.00
anish: 0-8170-1422-5 $16.00

sic Teacher Skills: A Handbook for Church School Teachers, Revised Edition
chard E. Rusbuldt   0-8170-1255-9 $12.00

aching Today's Teachers to Teach
onald L. Griggs   TETOTE $18.00

Ways to Become a Great Sunday School Teacher
lia Halverson   THTWWA $18.00

ALL GROUP MINISTRY RESOURCES

ading Small Groups: Basic Skills for Church and Community Organizations
than W. Turner   0-8170-1210-9 $13.00

sic Leader Skills: Handbook for Church Leaders
chard E. Rusbuldt   0-8170-0920-5 $12.00

om Group Publishing
he Encyclopedia of Practical Ideas" $24.99 each
all Group Ministry in the 21st Century   SMGR21
en's Ministry in the 21st Century   MEMI21
omen's Ministry in the 21st Century   WOMI21
uth Ministry in the 21st Century   YOMI21
ung Adult Ministry in the 21st Century   YOAD21

o order, call Judson Press at 800-458-3766,
order online at
ww.judsonpress.com.

JUDSON PRESS
PUBLISHERS SINCE 1824

Stimulating Small Group Discussion

Resources from Judson Press

THE GOSPEL ACCORDING TO DR. SEUSS LEADER'S GUIDE

Mark & Kate Ballard and Chester D. Williams

This study guide is designed to help readers discover the gospel themes foun◄ Judson's popular *The Gospel According to Dr. Seuss*. Includes six sessions ◄ questions and activities for use by teachers or leaders of four different age gro◄ young children, older children, youth, and adults.   978-0-8170-1498-8 $5.00

THE GOSPEL ACCORDING TO DR. SEUSS: Snitches, Sneetches, and Other Creachas

0-8170-1457-8 $10.00

LEFT BEHIND? The Facts Behind the Fiction: A Companion Guide

Cassandra Carkuff Williams

This small-group study guide explores alternative understandings of key Scrip◄ passages that have been linked to end-times events.   978-0-8170-1497-1 $5.0◄

LEFT BEHIND? The Facts Behind the Fiction

978-0-8170-1490-2 $14.00

DOWN BY THE RIVERSIDE: A Brief History of Baptist Faith Study Guide

Everett C. Goodwin

As a companion to *Down by the Riverside*, this new study guide provides eight sions that cover Baptist origins, how Baptists have organized in the United Sta and distinct expressions of Baptist faith. Includes questions for individual or gr◄ study. 978-0-8170-1496-9 $5.00

DOWN BY THE RIVERSIDE: A Brief History of Baptist Faith

0-8170-1400-4 $13.00

TO KNOW GOD: Small Group Exercises for Spiritual Formation

Michael Gemignani

Small group fellowship and spiritual formation come together to help readers e◄ rience God through the development of spiritual disciplines such as prayer, ◄ denial, study, meditation, and personal ministry.
0-8170-1394-6 $14.00

Call 800-458-3766, or save
20% when you order online at
www.judsonpress.com.

JUDSON PRES◄
PUBLISHERS SINCE 18◄